A Least Expected Heaven

HOMELESSNESS AND THE
SPIRITUALITY OF MEETING

D. CARL MAZZA

To Marsha

December 24, 1952 – May 12, 2008

a friend truly beyond my measuring

Dear Reader:

When I started writing this book, I kept pondering ways I could convince you I hadn't gone completely mad. Then, as I worked on it, I began to think, "Well, after all, it's about trust, isn't it? And commonality; and maybe things we all know, but can't easily talk about because it might just sound like some crazy idea we have in our heads." I mean, above all, we don't want to appear outlandish, do we? Consequently, I continued to write believing that there may be others out there who are also needing to pretend that they haven't lost their senses. For these, perchance, I thought this book might be good company, possibly even a prompt toward a deeper understanding of ourselves.

A lot of things are lost to us in life, but not a love which began before we were born. Our own story started in another time and place, a part of a much larger and longer journey. Our portion of that ongoing narrative is here and now, and our purpose is to extend the unfinished love, the legacy of who we are, among the people we meet along the way; and this "meeting" points to a heaven we least expected. Our own particular life is unlike any other. It's almost as if we're living to fulfill a solemn promise that we made long ago at a distant hearth, in an unremembered eon; a pledge which soundly grips the deepest part of who we are today as a person.

So, before you close this book, if I haven't already driven you completely away, read on a little, and see if the understandings of my life, different from yours surely, yet at their core perhaps remarkably similar, have not, in your experience, taught you much the same. If not, dear reader, I am grateful for your patience and I thank you for hearing me out.

Contents

One day a young fugitive, trying to hide himself from the enemy, entered a small village. The people were kind to him and offered him a place to stay. But when the soldiers who sought the fugitive asked where he was hiding, everyone became very fearful. The soldiers threatened to burn the village and kill every man in it unless the young man were handed over to them before dawn. The people went to the minister and asked him what to do. The minister, torn between handing over the boy to the enemy or having his people killed, withdrew to his room and read his Bible, hoping to find an answer before dawn. After many hours, in the early morning his eyes fell on these words: "It is better that one man dies than that the whole people be lost."

Then the minister closed the Bible, called the soldiers and told them where the boy was hidden. And after the soldiers led the fugitive away to be killed there was a feast in the village because the minister had saved the lives of the people. But the minister did not celebrate. Overcome with a deep sadness, he remained in his room. That night an angel came to him, and asked, "What have you done?" He said, "I handed over the fugitive to the enemy." Then the angel said: "But don't you know that you have handed over the Messiah?" "How could I know?" the minister replied anxiously. Then the angel said: "If, instead of reading your Bible, you had visited this young man just once and looked into his eyes, you would have known."

HENRI NOUWEN

Prologue

I am of second generation Italian descent, and the ideals of the old country and the *Risorgimento* are in my blood. Perhaps it is in my ancestors' uprooting, and the risky voyage they made from an old world to the new, that my lifelong identification with homelessness took root. From the instability of my own family, I traced my thoughts, even from earliest memory, into an attempt to understand the nature of home itself and what it means to belong.

From the age of sixteen, I have lived and worked in homeless missions and shelters, in New York City, Chicago, and Philadelphia. In 1981, following my ordination as a Presbyterian minister, I founded Meeting Ground in Cecil County, Maryland, along with my late wife Marsha, and for 30 years served this community with and among persons and families experiencing homelessness. It is from this background, and the people I have befriended over five decades, that this book is drawn.

Some years ago I found a book in a rather unexpected place. While browsing the library of Rev. Creighton Dunlap, the lifetime-embedded Pastor/Director of St. Paul's House in New York, an ultraconservative (I mean Victorian, literally) religious mission, I could scarcely believe my eyes when I saw a copy of Darwin's *Origin of Species*.

It was as shocking a find as a stack of Playboys at Osama bin Laden's. I knew Rev. Dunlap well; he was a friend and mentor to me at a turning point in my life. His quarrel with the *Origin* was as fierce and intense as the Anglican divines who decried its first publication. "What," I thought, "was this blatant heresy doing among his Bibles and sacred commentaries?"

The mystery unfolded somewhat when I turned the cover and read the comment he had handwritten in large letters on the title page: *"WARNING: DO NOT READ – This book has been proven false!"* Apparently he had been just as mystified as I to find Darwin somehow wangled among his devotionals, yet his staunch

Episcopalian heart couldn't bear the thought of throwing any book away, even one of such bald-faced error. And of course he couldn't have given it away either: that would have been like foisting a lie on the innocent or, for the already doubtful, like giving a copy of Jack London's *To Build a Fire* to an arsonist. I could see him brooding at his desk, the vile tome clutched in his hands, holding him captive in a mental pinball machine of impossible choices. Thus, the book went reluctantly back on the shelf, but with his stern admonition for anyone who, like me, might someday innocently come upon it.

I loved and respected the man who had taught me so much, but I wondered exactly why he was so fearful. Scared of an idea? Frightened perhaps that the challenge to his faith-system might prove effective? Why should anyone be afraid for their religion? With all its claims to be a window on absolute truth, can the structure of a religion be so flimsy as to fall apart when challenged by a new idea?

This question somehow summarizes my problem with so much of institutional religion as I have found it: how could there ever be a stairway to heaven in a house of such rigid, unbending cards? Heaven, as we might least expect, is rather to be gained, neither by fear nor by shopworn words, but by the boldness of our imagination unleashed as we meet ourselves and others in life. A living spirituality can't be based on fear of anything, but its strength is always in discovery, understanding, new being and a spirit of adventure with not a little curiosity. Spiritual demise doesn't happen because we ask questions, but begins rather when we are afraid to ask, and when we fail to be honest about ourselves and others. New ideas are not the death of religion, quite the opposite; just as the path to heaven itself is the vigor of our quest to find it.

This book is my personal exploration of the road to that place we call heaven. I know I'm juggling some ideas that can be subjective, obtuse and complicated, maybe beyond words to express adequately, and that's why I'm using true stories, close to my heart, to tell my tale. Hopefully they will be like windows on spiritual ideals which need to be, to me at least, uncomplicated, or, in the language of the physical sciences, expressed in ways that are simple, yet with a needed elegance for our lives.

While I say much in this book that is critical of institutional religion, I trust you to know that in reproaching religion, it's about my love, not my aversion. The fellowship of the Christian church has been the anchor of my life, and I have warm devotion for its forms and friendships. But institutions, even religious ones, need auditors to stay real. All true relationships have to face disillusionment, and when it happens—honesty is the best policy. So in our relationship to religion, friction is what deepens consciousness. What I want so passionately, and what many today yearn for, is a rekindling, a fresh imagination of who we are and what we are all about.

I'm not so high-minded as to think I'm proposing some grand scheme to change the world, but I also know I'm not alone in wanting to see the world changed. The world may ever be new, but it's not always so brave, especially in its devaluation of the individual human person. Any such dehumanization should compel us to be earnest in our desire to know each other, because intimacy and affection, not organized religion, is what makes us human. If religion has any purpose, it is not to be an end in itself, but always to inspire us to love all that is true of ourselves and others; and to be alive in the conviction that what humanity so urgently needs is the firm ground of real human meeting.

In the end, it's all about belonging, isn't it? At some level we're painfully aware of a nagging solitude—that perhaps we live unto ourselves and that even when we die, we're on our own. Yet, despite the tenacity of our loneliness, we sense, deep down, that we are never truly alone. Even as thoughts of our separateness press in on us, we remember that the eternal friendship we swore to each other as children was, in its nascent essence, an oath to life itself, and to our unshakable belonging to it all—along with the resplendent hope that, through all our years, we would never forget who we truly are.

Introduction:
Stories of the Sacred, Outside Religion

How long shall we sit in our porticoes practicing idle and musty virtues, which any work would make impertinent?

HENRY DAVID THOREAU, *Walden*

"What's on the other side?" I asked my uncle on a brilliant summer's day as we sat together on the beach. I was a boy of six; the year was 1953 and Wildwood was at that time a virtual Italian seaside colony in South Jersey on the road to renown as a rock-and-roll incubator and the *doo wop* capital of the western world. As children do, I was drawn away in thought as I dug handfuls of sand, gazing at the thin line where earth and sky meet. My first-generation Italian-American uncle was a short man with an enormous belly that to my young eyes looked like he swallowed a watermelon; everybody, including his wife, called him *Doc*. He was a dentist, but my mother said he was never to work on our teeth. I always knew he was doing well because he drove a Cadillac with all the bells and whistles like automatic windows, a big deal in the mid-1950's. Anyway, Uncle Doc was slumped in his sagging beach chair in his canvas hat, legs apart, engrossed in his newspaper while he chomped distractedly on the stub of a cigar. "Paris," he grunted without looking up and surely expressed with the hope that would end my questions, "Paris is what's on the other side." But I had expected him to say, *heaven.*

I thought it odd that my old uncle did not make that connection, which seemed so evident to me, and now I also wonder why he looked at the horizon and didn't think of his own roots, the distant shore of his ancestors. But he was an American

17

now who came of age in the postwar years of the 1920's: of course he might not think first of Italy. His parents, my grandparents, had boarded ship, watching as the last of their eternal homeland sank from view, even as they turned to embrace the unseen, irresistible coast of America. The risk they took was based on more than escape from an old life of static poverty. It was also a desire to travel to the distant shore, to discover another world, a better home.

I look back now, over a half-century, at the boy standing with his feet in the sand, hands cupped beside his eyes shielding them from the bright sun, gazing to the farthest reach of the sea, and I wonder if there is any child who has not done the same, and maybe also even dreamed that heaven might be there, somewhere on the far side of what the eye can see? I've long since been dispelled of the illusion that it's a place in France, but I've also come to realize that finding the place called heaven has been the defining dynamic of my life. Surprisingly what I have found has not been in the church, but outside institutional religion.

AT OUR LAST DAY, when every one of us is at that place where earth and sky convene, all that will matter will be how we grew in our lifetime, through all the relationships of our days, into the understanding of who we truly are. Spiritual discovery begins with the search to know ourselves and to recognize and meet ourselves in others. Anything less than this is surrender, a capitulation of our understanding of the divine to a ghost: a God who exists only on paper. At the outset, I'll say that I've lost faith in much of conventional religion, even as religion has played a huge role in my life. I don't think I'm alone in this. We humans are innately spiritual beings, and we won't settle forever for a standardized faith that maximizes the minimum, minimizes the maximum, and tolerates dishonesty and irrelevance. Even faithful religious people recognize this; I'm not saying anything new here. But I am saying that heaven must be found through the inspiration and insight of our loving relationships, and if this is not the heart of our religion, we need to look elsewhere.

I'm not out to debunk longstanding and well-worn organizational paths. Everyone needs some consolation in life, and if standardized religion is enough for you, nothing I say may be of any use. However, my own link to the eternal has been in my relationships with people, particularly persons who have experienced homelessness, and these sacred connections I've found in the unfolding of life itself. Our years don't have to be perceived as a chronology of events over time, like a world history exam. Rather, our lifetimes are like a voyage on which we discover each other. When we remember our lives, we remember people, not so much a sequence of events as those dazzling moments when we truly encounter: when we know we are deeply and inseparably connected to another person, however briefly. Through that divine link we know, we absolutely know, that we are connected to all life, every living thing, and this assurance of belonging extends even to the universe itself. It all begins with our relationships: to ourselves and all persons we meet. We are the revelation of the infinite to one another, mentors of the personality of God.

In the United States, so much of what passes today as Christian religion is vapid. And this is true for mainstream denominations as well as the glut of storefront, or should I say mall-front, churches, mega-churches, and televangelists that are popping up like rain-bogged mushrooms. While declining mainline churches are busy endlessly tweaking their organizational procedures, thriving churches *du jour* are fine-tuning the prosperity gospel, and what we know instinctively to be lacking in all, and urgently needed, is the creation of basic context for human meeting and a moral compass based on the knowledge of who we are—the true ground of our being: that all people are part of each other. Somehow, when we allow ourselves the time and space to move beyond our jumpy egos, the mask of our social life, we recognize that we are not isolated and self-contained beings. We simply know that we belong to one another.

Within and outside religion there is growing desire for a spirituality that works—having the capacity to transform our individual lives and renew society. While institutional houses of faith are everywhere, so is the growing uneasiness that all is not well: that we are drifting apart rather than together, and that we see more reason to fear the stranger than to embrace others as we would ourselves.

We need to know ourselves and each other before anything else, and this requires meeting. Our culture, whether for economic or political angst, is actively destroying these contexts of real encounter, isolating us as people, and creating haves and have-nots across the board. If the religious community does not see the spiritual famine in all this, it exists in a vacuum deeper than outer space. Religious institutions must be challenged continually or they run the risk of serving their structures and rules before a castaway humanity they profess to love. There is only one rule that really matters: meet yourself, meet your neighbor, love both sincerely and you will be one with God. Organized religion, particularly the mainline Church, is faced with the challenge to become a schoolhouse, not for instruction in reaching for a netherworld beyond the rainbow, but for human beings, in the multiplicity of their differences, who earnestly want to know themselves and meet each other now, here on earth. It's a potentially costly process, though. If any Church, any religious institution, dares become a catalyst for dynamic human neighborhood it will be countering a culture that will oppose it in blood. It may lose its life; it will be forever transformed—but in the end it will save its soul.

The homelessness which enveloped my childhood has never left me. To this day I carry with me always its tangible fears, defenses and anxieties. Among the thousands of persons I have known who have been homeless, I have encountered a spirituality of meeting which I have rarely found in the Church. This book is my attempt to convey what I have been taught. And for those who have instructed me so well, my hope is that the stories of this book will confirm the consolation that even in the chaos of homelessness a person is never truly alone. We owe this confidence to one another because we all have, in like way, been encouraged through life by the kind and simple honesty of others.

Perhaps, also, those who consider themselves outsiders, especially who find themselves increasingly outside religion, will take some heart in what I write. I know that when I use the term *outsiders* I am somehow violating the heart of my own thesis—that of our ultimate *oneness* as people. A better term might be something like seekers, but that word doesn't quite do it. I am addressing persons who, like me, feel they are on a life quest to find home: a place of true belonging. So, it might be more accurate for me to say: *persons who feel like outsiders*. These are persons who resolve truth more in the stream of action than by deliberation. They decide by doing, and form new principles and realities based on their relationships with others. Perhaps they are, by life experience or membership, connected to a religion, but their real sanctuary is the spirituality of the deed. They act on the conviction that true words and righteous actions are inseparable, that beliefs not acted upon are hollow. Theirs is the service of a deep intuition of life and the oneness of all living; that one's life is important to all others and in keeping covenant with generations yet unborn to plant, by our actions in the present, the seed corn of our future.

I THINK OF THIS BOOK AS A JOURNEY. At Meeting Ground we once gave hospitality to a man from India who was in the middle of a peace-walk around the world. He had some distant relation to Gandhi, although I can't recall how exactly. What I do clearly remember was his Gandhi-like aura, especially impressive to peace-movement Americans—so we tended to pay special attention to what he said, like Presbyterians perking to a Scottish brogue. When I asked him why he had undertaken such an ambitious three-year project he explained, "My walk isn't from place to place, it's from person to person: that's how I'm meeting you." He might have said the same about the journey of life itself; life is the spirituality of meeting, ourselves and others, and we write the sacred book, page by page, from person to person.

This book is my walk, or, more appropriately, my voyage to you; at least it is my high hope I will be able to make that connection. The stories are about people I have known who, like me, have experienced the grief of homelessness. I chose them out of many others I could tell, because, taken together, they best describe what I mean by the spirituality of meeting, each one relaying a part of it, and each one pointing to a least expected heaven. All have instructed me through their living, giving me a window into the anatomy of the spirit side of life and, dare I say, even the arc of the cosmos itself. In the pages that follow, I would be glad to know that, in some small way, they have reached you also.

The Spirituality of Meeting

Jesus said: Love thy brother [and sister] as thy soul; keep him as the apple of thine eye.

THE GOSPEL OF THOMAS, 25

It was sub-zero, a dark and bitter cold night sometime around 1978; it was late and I was driving on an unfamiliar road in upstate New York with my tank on empty: definitely not a time to run out of gas, especially in the middle of nowhere. The wind was brutal, and the chill so intense that skin could freeze on any touch to metal. I finally saw the lights of a gas station and pulled up to the pump with a huge sigh of relief. It was full-service only, more expensive for that plus being out in the sticks, but on this night it was no problem for me to pay a little more to stay warm inside the car.

As I stopped my engine, the attendant popped out of a heated stall, like toast from a toaster, quick-stepping over to my car. He was young, probably a high school kid I thought, wearing a flimsy jacket and knitted hat pulled down over his ears, his hands crammed stiffly in his pants pockets; he was obviously not prepared for the cold. I rolled the window down just enough to blurt out what I wanted, and just as quickly rolled it right back up as he reached for the pump. I watched from my side mirror and saw that he didn't have any gloves; he was using an old rag to keep his hands from freezing, struggling to hold the metal handle. He was in trouble. Even with the rag he couldn't manage to get the nozzle in my tank: it kept dropping to the ground as his hand touched it.

I instinctively fumbled under my seat for an old pair of gloves I kept there and handed them out the window to him. He stood stone still for a moment, looking at me so deliberately and

23

intently I felt I had done something wrong: maybe I had insulted him by offering to help, implying he wasn't prepared for his job or that I considered him a charity case, or whatever.

But just as quickly his surprised expression changed to a soft, almost radiant gratitude; I will never forget that look as he readily accepted the gloves and put them on with obvious relief. In that brief exchange something sincere passed between us, like an understanding that went beyond words. We didn't say anything, except I insisted, against his protests, that he keep the gloves. As I drove away, looking back through the rear-view mirror, I just caught sight as he charged back into his warm space, and I felt a surge of light-headed happiness. What had happened? My act of giving was not so much generosity, more like impulse. The gloves were my old ones; I didn't give away my good pair, so it cost me nothing and didn't change my lifestyle in the least. Yet, his response, his open gratitude, was so marked and vivid as if my gift had been some heroic act. It could be that he was just plain happy to have something that would stand between him and frostbite that night.

When I was in college I worked a summer for the Stratford Cookson Company, a dental equipment factory in Yeadon, Pennsylvania. At lunch one day a woman who had been there for decades, angrily confronted a male co-worker who had made a smirking racial slur while casually taking a bite out of the corner of his sandwich. She put her own sandwich down like a person would quick-flip a Frisbee onto the table, slowly standing to her feet with a steady, angry glare and in a measured Irish cadence told him how she had been riding the bus to work every day, standing, waiting at the stop in the early-morning cold, "For years," her voice rose in an unyielding meter, "for years those other women, the ones you just insulted, stood there too, like me," as she pushed her rolled fist into her chest, "like me, on their way to work, and I knew they were just as cold as I was." There were no more ethnic smears at the table that day.

There's something about the cold that strips away our pretense to feel separate from other people, or even from animals for that matter; we even make sure our plants are protected. It reduces our life to an elemental need and we are given a short window to see ourselves as we are, made of the same stuff as everybody else. My co-worker knew that in her heart: not from ideology, but from meeting others who stood with her on many a cold morning. Just like stopping for gas on a freezing winter's night didn't make me a new person—it just made me remember, for that second, who I really was.

THE GREAT DUAL COMMANDMENT of the Christian religion has similar echo in all faiths: *"Love the Lord your God with all your heart and with all your soul and with all your mind and with all your strength. The second is this: Love your neighbor as yourself. There is no commandment greater than these."* (Mark 12:29-31NIV). In this passage we see that the whole of our identity—heart, soul, mind, and body—is summoned to *love God.* The love of God is bound here, tied to who we are, making our knowledge of self the pathway to knowing the divine. They are so closely intertwined that we might easily conclude that to do one is to accomplish the other, but at a minimum we are awake to the fact that if we want to love God we must do it by knowing who we are and all that we are. *"Once, having been asked by the Pharisees when the kingdom of God would come, Jesus replied, The kingdom of God does not come with your careful observation, nor will people say, 'Here it is,' or 'there it is,' because the kingdom of God is within you."* (Luke 17:20, 21) It doesn't get much more direct than that.

The second part of the commandment links our love of neighbor to the love we have for ourselves. As we meet God by honestly knowing ourselves, so it is also true that we comprehend the divine when we truly meet our neighbor—not in the general affection for humankind, but in the particular—the one who is near to us. If God is transcendent, unknown and unknowable, except perhaps by some self-avowed special revelation, how then can we learn to love what or who we can't know? There is no God in the sky; walls do not define the margins of deity, nor do words, nor even a religion. The revolutionary heart of Jesus' teaching was so altogether different: if we want to know God we must do so in loving meeting with ourselves and others.

Remarkably, when Jesus taught what God is like he did it, not by expounding some mystical private knowledge, but by telling stories about people—linking the intimate details of their lives to ours. He explained the nature of the infinite in the ordinary ways of a farmer, a corrupt judge, a parent, a shepherd, a compassionate traveler, a landlord, an old impoverished woman, a builder, a man lavishly rich and one grotesquely poor, priests, debtors, brides and grooms, ungrateful children, a lawyer, and even a white-collar criminal. He put it simply: to meet God, meet yourself in your neighbor and in these encounters learn those qualities, strengths, and weaknesses inherent in the human soul that stretch beyond the finite.

This meeting is not the everyday polite encounter, exchanging pleasantries and casual talk, nor the defensive relationships for which we have prepared and steeled ourselves; rather, it is the meaningful face-to-face engagement of an *I-thou* relationship, understanding, as Martin Buber has written, "a person cannot approach the divine by reaching beyond the human." Meeting is to recognize in another that which, as we have seen in ourselves, is an expression of God, our oneness with all that is living. The great commandment is all about meeting.

Ham-fisted Religion

Where does organized religion go wrong? In the early 1990's, I was helping to serve an early morning Sunday breakfast, attended mainly by homeless folks, in the basement of a large Wilmington, Delaware church. About 150 persons were gathered for eggs, coffee and all the trimmings. It was a chilly, crisp fall day, and the fellowship was warm and welcome. While the meal was going on downstairs, preparations were underway upstairs in the sanctuary for a worship service. We were almost done and starting to clean up while folks lingered around coffee. I happened to be sweeping the floor in front of a small elevator that connected the kitchen area to the main church above. I heard it descending with a grinding base-hum, thudding to a stop. The door opened and a cleric appeared, fully robed in black and white cassock and surplice, red chasuble and multicolored stole, like a plumed bird, presumably a bishop or among that order. I felt myself resisting the urge to genuflect. He stepped one foot out, keeping the other in the elevator and one hand tightly holding open the door; his anxious eyes glancing rapidly, first to me then to the breakfast gathering, then back to me. I knew something was wrong.

"Who's in charge?" he asked as he waved his fully-dressed arm toward the meal like a bat's wing unfolding, "Who's in charge here? Who's responsible for this?" Mustering the courage to admit some ownership I replied, "I guess you can talk to me." "Okay," he said, gesturing again with an open wing toward the gathering, "when are you going to get these people out of here? We're getting ready for service upstairs; we can hear the noise."

Again, rather uneasily, and I confess with a manufactured deference to his authority, I replied that we were doing our best, but that, for some, it was the only warm place they would have for most of the day and we were not in a great hurry to rush them outside. There followed an awkward and too-long pause, his eyes fastened uncomfortably on mine. What could he say? Clearly he wasn't satisfied. "We're happy to have them for breakfast," he replied, "but in the future we *do* expect them to be out by the time *church* starts." With another quick, displeased glare toward the gathering, he folded himself back into the elevator, made a final, semi-annoyed eye contact with me, shut the door, and rose with a grinding rumble to the region above.

As I stood there, broom in hand, I ruminated on my now-dispelled presumption that *church* was always a place where a multitude of strangers would be heartily welcome and especially those poor or disenfranchised. "Such is the life of a transcendent God," I thought, "cloistered upstairs, disturbed by the muffled voices of outsiders seeping through the masonry." I don't name that particular church, mainly because it doesn't deserve to be singled out like that. Like many churches, it wasn't into a pattern of casually ignoring strangers in its midst, but also like many others it could lapse too easily into a mission of *doing for others* rather than *being with others*.

Gandhi's famous too-often quoted, *"You must be the change you want to see in the world"* says it well, but it isn't said any better than by Jesus when he was eating dinner at his friend Lazarus' house. Martha was consumed with preparing a meal for her guest, a thoroughly laudable and sacrificial act. To be perfectly honest, I can't see anything wrong with Martha's single-minded commitment to the task; at least she was trying. But it came unraveled because she made it all about the *doing*. Distracted even from herself, she brusquely demanded that Jesus cut off his conversation with Mary so she could help her cook. She was testy to the point of anger with her sister as well as her eminent, but blithely male nevertheless, house guest. For Jesus though, it was all about a meeting-point: the practice of just *being* by coming-together. Risking insult to his host, he made it clear to Martha that Mary had chosen the *better part* by simply sitting with him for a while. Martha was feeding dinner, but Mary, at a grave time for Jesus, was embracing a man hungry for life in the face of his looming death. [Luke 10:38-42] What is the mission of organized religion if not to add endearment to all human relationships, especially in its reach to those it considers outsiders? Serving others is not so much doing something for them as it is being together in the possibility of truly meeting one another. If being is not the core of mission, there is no mission. Religion is not about doing worship, even in the performance of holy services, but like Mary's better part, it is to be worship—present with and among others.

IN HIS CLASSIC WORK about the nature of community in the United States, *Bowling Alone*, Harvard professor Robert D. Putnam describes what he calls, *the ominous plunge in social connectedness.* He argues that, *as we enter a new century... it is now past time to reweave the fabric of our communities.* What's needed to do this is what he calls *bridging social capital*: acts of meeting which transcend *our social and political and professional identities to connect with people unlike ourselves.* Putnam concludes that the reform of society simply will not happen *unless you and I reconnect with our friends and neighbors.* Yet, with all the built in potential it has to do this critical work and meet this challenge, Putnam concludes that the Church is instead adding to the problem:

> *...as the 21st century opens Americans are going to church less often than we did three or four decades ago, and the churches we go to are less engaged with the wider community. Trends in religious life reinforce rather than counterbalance the ominous plunge in social connectedness in the secular community. (Putnam, 2000: p. 79)*

Putnam's sobering analysis was published in 2000, well before 9/11 and before the financial collapse of 2008. The first decade of the 21st century was shock-and-awe: a dramatic intensification of the need for this social capital. The economic, political, and social realities of the second decade are those of widespread polarization: red vs. blue, haves vs. have-nots, 1% vs. 99%, Tea Party vs. Occupy Movement, and, in the age of terrorism, the unimaginable return of barbarians at the gates. It's all closing in to make us more divided, more fearful, and less one as people–assailing any presumption that our race is fashioned in any manner of divinity: relentlessly obliterating who we are.

Most presidential inaugural speeches aren't well remembered, but John Kennedy's was different. Many vividly recall the sunny, frozen January day when he inspired the nation with the extraordinary summons, "Here on earth, God's work must truly be our own." The words, enshrined on his tomb at Arlington, were spoken to challenge everyone, religious or not, and they rightly assume that organized religion and religious people don't have a monopoly on God's work, even given religion's propensity to define everything it undertakes that way. But what exactly is

God's work? Surely though, for religion, for the church, it is the unique task to make humanity human—to defy economic and social barriers, including the ossifying gap between rich and poor, which prevent our meeting and embracing as a people, and to create the justice of human neighborhood, what Martin Luther King, Jr. called *the beloved community.* Not to engage this work fully is at best a catastrophic failure of any church. At worst it is the *Spiritus Immundus*: the unclean, unpardonable sin of our age.

Don't get me wrong about religion: even at its worst, organized religion, the church, can serve a charitable and soothing purpose, and far be it from me to deny anyone that. And many individual communities, whether outwardly religious or not, strive to practice the spirituality of meeting. But inasmuch as religion puts the needs of the institution before anything else, cloaking its highhandedness in syrupy ecclesiastical justification and relying on miracle, mystery, and authority like the taciturn Grand Inquisitor of the Brothers Karamazov—it is moribund. On the other hand, as it gives expression to our common vulnerability, as it opens us to dialogue of the heart, as it provides for us to like our enemies as well as ourselves, as it inspires the boldness of the deed on our own responsibility—it can serve us well on the voyage that we must make: from an old world to the new, the place called heaven. But I don't want to talk so much about the shortcomings of religion. We hunger for the spirituality of meeting, and what follows is my attempt to describe that as best as I can, as I have learned it from people I have come to know.

Another Country

I offer neither pay, nor quarters, nor food; I offer only hunger, thirst, forced marches, battles and death. Let him who loves his country with his heart, and not merely with his lips, follow me... I offer this word with deepest affection and from the very bottom of my heart.

GIUSEPPE GARIBALDI

There is in all of us a passion to make our mark, to be remembered for who we were and what we hoped for. That passion was in the mind of my ancestors when they traded their bucolic ancient home in Southern Italy for the concrete, chaotic streets of South Philadelphia. Their mission was that their children would inherit a world of possibility unknown in Europe. What we strive to leave behind for others through our moment of life is the fibrous tissue of our soul. Our everyday relationships may not seem extraordinary for the most part, but none of us stands alone. We are heirs and progenitors of a larger self, a heritage from those who went before us that we continue in our lifetime, hoping the best of it will survive us as the birthright of others.

In the mid-19th century, Italy was captivated by the *Risorgimento* (resurgence), a spontaneous and electric movement for national unity and liberty from foreign domination. The peninsula had been divided for centuries into independent and semi-autonomous city states, often warring among themselves and competing for preeminence. Now, in a sudden burst of awakening, heroic figures appeared: none more compelling than Giuseppe Garibaldi who strode like a red-shirted colossus over the Italian soul, marching his legions under the banner of a new birth of freedom. The *Risorgimento* was fluid and dynamic, appealing to the passion of oneness and the love of community: all Italians bound in a common identity they hadn't known perhaps since the days of ancient Rome—humanity no longer seen as a collection of bickering clans, but as a single family. It stirred a spirit of adventure in a young landlocked generation who now saw the possibility of a life larger than that of their parents. Their hearts swelled with the pride of this imagination; they were challenged to seek the prosperity of a world suddenly made so much bigger and more accessible. The ocean was no longer a forbidding barrier; it was now viewed as a pathway to the horizon and beyond. The risk of their transformation was now at hand.

I've think I inherited my own struggle with rootlessness from my grandparents. They started to come to America in the years after the American Civil War, still immersed in the turbulent spirit of their own cultural resurgence. My great grandfather Alessandro Colacchi was the first to come over, around 1885. He settled in the teeming South Philadelphia neighborhood around 9th and Christian Streets, now the landmark Italian Market. It was a crowded community of vendor stalls, restaurants, push carts, and row homes dominated by a large ramshackle boarding house for new arrivals. For the most part, those in my family who came over were shopkeepers and artisans, but in this New World the next generation followed a different drummer.

Both my maternal grandparents were born in Italy and came to America through Castle Garden, before Ellis Island had even been established as an intake center. My grandfather, Angelo Tierno, a rather shadowy figure in the family history, was a barber who after fathering nine daughters and a son in two decades, became a solitary visitor in and out of the home, until his wife Rosa, a teenager when she married, tired of his careening, considered him as good as dead, although he lived another 20 years. (My grandmother decided to start calling herself a widow, an interesting foil around the Roman Catholic Church's ban on divorce.)

My mother was baptized *Carmella*, but always known by her Americanized name Millie. She was born in 1910, the seventh of ten children, and came of age in the years just after the First

World War. Her early passion was music, and in the Jazz Era of the 1920's she developed a singular talent for the piano. While she was still a teenager, she was a sought-after accompanist for the silent movies. She loved the songs from the First World War, and one of my fondest memories growing up was sitting by the piano, my mother at her happiest, listening to her endlessly playing songs like, *Over There*, and *What Are You Going to Do for Uncle Sammy?* I remember seeing an old grade school picture of her with her class: she was tall, willowy as they used to say, her eyes and mischievous smile exuding the excitement of life in the Promised Land. I always felt so fortunate to have that brief glimpse into the soul of someone I came to know in a much different way.

My father's extended family, a clan full of musicians, emigrated *en masse* from Naples at the turn of the 20th century. They all pursued a typical pattern—husband and father first, followed a year or two later by mother and small children. By then all were coming through Ellis Island in New York as few ships from Europe made direct passage to Philadelphia. I was named after my paternal grandfather, Carlo Mazza, an import merchant and musician. He was a man at home on two continents, and while olive oil and foodstuffs were his livelihood, music was his passion, and he passed this love to his sons, even his in-laws: many of them devoted their lives to it as a result of his influence. It's been a mystery to me that only my mother, out of 10 children and countless other relations, gave her life to music; many of the rest of her family were self-made entrepreneurs, involved in everything from a fruit stand and hoagie shop to property rentals. Both sides of the family had an unquenchable thirst for their children to go to college; they were artistic, earthy, and upwardly mobile—a pretty fair summary of the Italian experience in America.

My father, christened *Vincenzo* but always known as Vince, was born in 1907, three years before my mother. My parents met on the vibrant streets of that Little Italy and formed their friendship around their exceptional talent for music. Like my mother, my father began working as a teenager, playing in nightclub bands in Philadelphia and South Jersey. Their letters from the time reveal some of the turbulence of their budding relationship, in part as a result of their difficult struggle, like many of their generation, to merge into the mainstream culture. The infamous trial and execution of *Nicola Sacco* and *Bartolommeo Vanzetti* in the 1920's, sparking vehement worldwide protests, defined the era for many as Italian-Americans fought to move beyond societal prejudice and stereotyping to prosper as citizens in their own right.

After going together for a decade, my parents married in 1934 at the height of the Great Depression. Finding success in their careers, in the midst of hard times, and following the general migration of their peers, they stepped-up and moved to a less crowded South Philadelphia neighborhood. I was born in December, 1946, a middle child between two brothers, at Philadelphia Hospital, the oldest in the country, boasting Benjamin Franklin as its founder. The following year my parents made their big move outside the city to the near western suburb of Upper Darby, and, sadly, that's when our family began slowly to disintegrate. Our home life there was relatively stable at first, but by the time I was in school my parents had separated. My father just left, walked out, and returned to live in the old city neighborhood to work as a musician and music teacher. I never knew completely why he left, but I always suspected that life's growing responsibilities, along with the cultural shock of 1950's suburbia, just plain scared him back to a life as a solitary country *Paisano*.

Whatever the reason, after his departure my mother found it increasingly difficult to cope with her isolated and overextended life, transplanted into a still largely unfamiliar and alien middle-class, two-parent society. She tried to work as a beautician, eventually opening her own shop, but it was short-lived. As a child, I was most in fear of losing our home as I watched her struggling, even under the burden of her increasing mental illness, to keep it all together. I could feel her fear, but we were never able to talk about it. The priest from the local parish came once. I'm sure he saw our predicament; he had us all kneel in the living room. He waved his hand over us, said a blessing in Latin, and left. I never saw him again. After he was gone we just went on before with the embarrassment of having to wear the same clothes every

34

day, times of little food, and fighting anxiously, constantly, to maintain the family *secret*. Following the illness and death of my younger sister in 1961, life pressed an emotional burden on top of an already tightening financial vise and my mother's mental health disintegrated along with the unrepaired house. Our world became a declining melodrama of debt collectors, sheriff sales, and increasing poverty. In 1962, my mother was committed, against her will, to Haverford State Mental Hospital.

My younger brother, Roger, and I continued to live in the house by ourselves, and I thought we could make it work just fine, at least until our mother could get released from the hospital. The health department didn't agree, though, nor did the sheriff. I came home from school one day to find my brother sitting on the front porch with a look of downright fear I'll never forget. The house was padlocked with a sign on the door forbidding entry—unsafe and unhealthy—and thus our homeless odyssey began. Of course it wasn't called homelessness in those days, but I suppose a rose of any other name... Suddenly the world looked so different. Everyone, except us, I thought, had a home—a secure place to go at the end of the day. Everyone, except us, I thought, belonged somewhere—and knew they belonged. What I remember so clearly even now is how quickly everything changed; how the world suddenly seemed inside, and we outside and alone: like it was just happening to us, only us, and we should be ashamed. And there was no light at the end of the tunnel, and for that matter sometimes there was no tunnel even. A couple of my aunts, my mother's sisters, did what they could to help; my brother and I were passed from one place to another and sometimes we had no place at all. I still carry with me the grief of our homelessness from those days.

Roger was 14 months younger than me; he never fully recovered from the shock of the events that left us homeless. All of his adult life was spent focused on maintaining the security of a tiny rundown efficiency apartment which he held onto through hell and high water (*aka* exorbitant rent), clinging for the security of it, afraid even to think of moving. I lost touch with him in the last months of his life, not realizing that he again became homeless. Looking back, I think it must have been the shame of being evicted from his carefully hoarded apartment that made him just give up and decide to drop off the map: no one knew where he was or how to reach him. He resurfaced when the Delaware County (PA) hospital called to tell me that he was there and "a very sick man." Relieved finally to be back in touch, I went to see him and found out that he had been living on the streets and in shelters for several months, and doing little to take care of himself. He never left the hospital. At age 47, the saga of his homelessness ended in that place.

SOMETIME AROUND 1961, when my mother was struggling alone to provide and keep us together, some well-meaning and anonymous persons arranged for a local grocer to deliver a food box to our house. They never knocked; we only discovered it when we were about to go out one day, sitting on the back doorstep like a newborn with a note. It had been there awhile; I could tell because the lunch meat was warm and starting to spoil. Nevertheless, it was a welcome sight to me as we needed food, although I thought the choice of groceries was weird. But I was decidedly not happy to see my mother's reaction. I'll never forget it. When she saw the box, she cried—not for any happiness but for the shame that others thought of her as a charity case. She let us eat the food, but she herself would have none of it. Another box arrived in a few days, and this time the ire of her old self was fully aroused; she called the store to tell them in a few salted words to stop the deliveries. They did. I remember thinking that doubtless her well-meaning benefactors would be offended, especially after they were told about her phone call, and with not even a *thank you* from us for their efforts. But we experienced it all quite differently. If those who meant to do good felt any satisfaction, pleasure, or wisdom in their efforts it was unwittingly at the expense of pain to my mother and through her to me.

Helping others in time of need is at my core, even my life's work, and the urge to help is what makes humanity humane. But I learned as a child, on the other side of charity, that the act of giving is not complete, and may do more harm than help, unless there is the opportunity to allow a gift in return and with it the esteem in which the relationship, and the person, is held.

In the midst of the bedlam of a disintegrating home, I learned something about organized religion that changed the course of my life. To my family in its distress, the local Roman Catholic Church, which my mother had attended loyally, which memories stand out from my childhood as heels clicking on terrazzo floors, mesmerizing stained glass windows, dreamy statues, rows and rows of lighted candles, and priests dressed in togas—offered no tangible help to my family in its devastating downward drift. Beyond the mystery and miracles we desperately needed the ministration of life, the security of belonging which had slipped from our grasp. I decided I didn't want any more part of this *religion* when I was fourteen, at my grandmother's funeral.

My mother and her sisters were in violent disagreement (most of us Italians have that personality disorder) on where to bury their mother and because of this they laid her to rest in a temporary crypt. It was a large underground cavernous place, basically a long-term morgue, but it acted like an echo chamber, amplifying any noise, even a whisper. You have to imagine what it sounded like when the funeral cortege gathered in that confined space and the wailing began. In an effort to calm things, the priest put his hand on my mother's shoulder while she sobbed inconsolably and, trying to be heard above the din, he spoke right into her ear, "Please, please don't be sad; your mother's in heaven now…" "… Oh, Really?!" I thought, "Did it work that fast?"— recalling the church had just finished selling prayer cards to the family to get their mother on the fast-track out of purgatory. I understood he was just trying to offer consolation, but I couldn't help but wonder if he had just pulled a fast one. Even at my tender age, I perceived it was an interesting way to make money and it was my tipping point: I'd had enough of a commercialized God; they lost me—mind, heart, and soul.

IT WAS AT THIS TIME, around 1962, through a nearby Presbyterian Church, that I met some people who were in the institution but not its hired guns. Had they acted more Presbyterian I probably would have kept my distance; my religious upbringing included stern warnings about the eternal danger of associating with Protestants. I had been in the basement of a Presbyterian church once for some Cub Scout meetings, but I was strictly forbidden to attend the service upstairs for Scout Recognition Sunday. Although by the time I was a young teenager I had lost interest in any religion, I liked these Presbyterians because they seemed interested in me as a person rather than as a mission project. Theirs was not the cause, the program, or the convert; they were looking for their own moorings in life and welcomed me to be with them in their own search and discovery.

Their leader was Bill Eisenhuth, a thirty-something cab driver who was converted to Christianity in a movie theater during a showing of *Ben Hur*. His assistant was Charlie Dennis who was disabled from advanced stage Multiple Sclerosis, from which he died a few years later. All the other members of the group were in high school or college, some from different churches, but most were like me, feeling disconnected from church and religion.

One of the members of this special group of seekers and misfits was Todd Rundgren who went on to fame and fortune as a world renowned musician and songwriter. I remember many happy times when we used to gather around Todd as he played the church piano. He would hunch over the keys, his hands lifting high and working the ivories like someone lightly touching fingertips to a pan of hot dish water, totally engrossed in an original musical style that foreshadowed his fame. Even then I perceived a strong spiritual yearning in his songs, a quest for honesty in relationships. He and the other friends I met in that pack of outsiders granted to me and my family a sanction: permission to grieve our fall and move on. It was through them I first discovered that the sacred, the spirit of God, was not an ecclesiastical monopoly, but was everywhere present in and among people, if not more likely so, outside religion.

The church that hosted the group, Trinity Presbyterian in Clifton Heights, Pennsylvania, was theologically conservative and old-school; I assimilated their customs and ways because I felt human with them, but their particular brand of theology was incidental to the door they opened to knowing myself and who I really was apart from my socially humiliating circumstances. There was really nothing in the church that was sacred to me except the relationships I formed; friendships that made it clear to me that if I wanted to find heaven I would have to quit looking up at the sky.

MY MOTHER WAS BETTER for a time after her release from the hospital sometime in 1963, but she still struggled hard to maintain a semblance of home for the rest of her life. She was strong-willed and fiercely independent. To the end she preferred to live at times without heat or electricity, even in a tent, so that she could know she was coping by her own means and not depending on others. She taught me, by her example, so much about the human spirit and its thirst for freedom and dignity. Her sharp sense of humor, especially reserved for poking the pompous asses she did not suffer gladly, stayed intact through the toughest times, as did her down-to-earth, one-of-a-kind disposition. I once noticed a hacksaw sitting on the back seat of her old car and offhandedly asked about it.

"Oh, that," she said, "I keep it in the car in case I have an accident.

"Uh… I still don't get it, what happens in an accident?"

"So I can saw my way out," she replied.

She died in 1983, suddenly after a stroke. Although my home life growing up had been one long bout with insecurity and dread, my mother's passing left me with a loneliness I hadn't expected, and a realization, fuller that I ever knew, of how much her love had anchored me in life—more than any religious benediction or sacrament. Such devout ceremonies surely have their place, in some lives more than others, but even their most sublime expression can never begin to compare with the irreplaceable sovereignty of unconditional human affection in a person's life: surely our most direct union to that which is divine.

IT WAS ESPECIALLY IN NEW YORK CITY, at St. Paul's House Mission in the Hell's Kitchen neighborhood of Manhattan's west side, that I began to learn the stories that became sacred to me in my road to finding heaven. I was sixteen years old when I first lived there in the summer of 1963. I made a lot of friends like Mario Lozano, who was my age, from a Puerto Rican family living nearby. We would get together and take long walks around the city, just to talk. Sometimes in the evening we would go to a bakery when the new bread was coming out of the ovens, and we'd sit on a stoop sharing an enormous French loaf while talking far into the night. He used to talk about his family being so poor; for him was like being in a box. By the time he was old enough to know what was happening, he felt irrevocably trapped. Barriers of race and culture, family struggling daily just to survive, episodic education in bad schools—all were his birthright. He considered the dreams of youth to be more like illusions, ever drifting in a vague hopelessness for the future. Already far behind his peers in seizing opportunity, he wondered how he could ever compete to fulfill his ambition of becoming a commercial airline pilot in the well-heeled, well-educated world.

The themes of home and homelessness started to become important to me in my understanding of earth and heaven. I first noticed the example set by the great masters in their times as landless sojourners. Jesus' retreat in the wilderness, not unlike Buddha's escape into the dark woods, led to the focusing of their own spiritual minds. They saw all people as of one kindred. Both Jesus and Buddha sought to re-create fatherhood and motherhood as the ground of being which unites all in one truehearted family. Under this arrangement, human beings become sisters and brothers and no one, truly, should ever lack a home, a place of belonging— for body as well as soul.

AS A YOUNG MAN in my teens and early twenties, during the turbulent 1960's, I lived alternately in York City, Chicago, and Philadelphia. I didn't have any money for college, but I wanted to go more than anything. As if I hadn't by now had enough trouble with religion, when I heard that tuition was free at Moody Bible Institute in Chicago, I decided it was as good a place as any to get my start. I enrolled there in 1964. For whatever reason, I didn't realize that I had already come too far seriously to assimilate what they were teaching, and as a result I struggled through three years of pious nonsense—such as their prohibition of inter-racial dating based on an esoteric interpretation of the book of Genesis. Dodging rules and closing my eyes to a multitude of holy inconsistencies, I made it to graduation in 1967 by the skin of my teeth. I survived and continued there only because I was actually rooted elsewhere: at the nearby Gospel League Home, a rescue mission at the edge of the old Skid Row district on Chicago's Near Northwest Side. It was a sprawling building, a former 19th century settlement house turned shelter for what they called, in those days, *stranded* families. Through this and other old-time-religion lighthouses—feeding stations with pulpits, giving out baloney sandwiches for church attendance—I came to relish an earthy, street-level warmth with others who also had deep unspoken life-warping secrets. I came to know poverty and alienation from new perspectives, different from my broken immigrant home, and I began to realize that there were many other reasons for homelessness. In these missions and storefront churches I became part of another kind of family, and in these I began fully to understand the *spirituality of meeting*.

I SPENT THE SUMMER OF 1967 working under the Presbyterian Evangelistic Committee at the Church of the Evangel in South Philadelphia. The once burgeoning starched Scotch-Irish congregation was down to around 25 members in the middle of an African-American neighborhood. The part-time pastor was a pleasant retired gentleman with a lush mane of bright white hair. He was like the aged building, a noble vestige of a bygone era, and also like the congregation itself, a handful of old commuters who had grown up in the church a half century earlier but who had long since moved far away from their old neighborhood. The Sunday service was like a time warp back to that era. In a rhythm like the beat of an institutional clock, the kind I remembered from high school, announcing each new interminable minute of a stifling class with a loud click and tiny shift of its hand, inching like a slug in winter to the merciful hour of dismissal, so at Evangel, in methodical measure, everything moved in an endless slow motion. Listening carefully, in that dark oak-paneled sanctuary, one could almost hear, as bottoms shifted restlessly in the pews, the chant of a grand somnambulatory chorus reflexively singing: *good fences make good neighbors.*

I had heard about the church and I asked to be assigned there for the summer, although against the advice of the Presbytery committee that ran the program. Perceiving my evangelical leaning, they preferred that I cut my eyeteeth with the denomination in a larger, well administered, successfully integrated West Philadelphia parish. But at Evangel I knew there was a dedicated retired woman of hearty Scottish descent, Hannah McFetridge, a diamond in the rough, who had single-handedly developed a blossoming Sunday school and youth program. She had scores of young people, sometimes numbering in the hundreds, coming to a spirited youth gathering at the church every Saturday night. I wanted to spend my summer helping and learning from her, so, against advice, I went over, introduced myself and got started; the Committee grudgingly gave in, went along, and let me do it, much to their later regret.

Like the neighborhood itself, the church was sharply divided: white Sunday morning drive-from-out-of-town worshipers on one side, and black neighborhood youth Fellowship on the other, and the two never mixed or met. Hannah was waging a lonely one-woman battle to introduce a young African-American pastor to change the entire tenor of Sunday morning and attract new blood to the church, but the elders would have none of it.

The South Philadelphia neighborhood around 18th and Tasker streets, where Evangel Church was located, was in transition, on top of the fact that it was a turbulent, long-hot-summer in the Civil Rights era. Formerly a solidly white middle class enclave, the community was more lower-income mow with a growing number of Italian and African Americans. The two

42

communities lived, or rather coexisted, side-by-side with no social interchange, the streets themselves serving literally as boundary lines: all of one race on one side, all of another across the street.

Things reached a sudden crisis at the church one fine Sunday morning in August. The Fellowship Hall, which on Saturday nights rocked with band music, food, and excitement, converted back on Sunday morning to its traditional use as the home of, you guessed it, the all-white adult Sunday school class. On this morning Mrs. Hannah, as the young people respectfully called her, was working at a small desk in the corner while the dozen or so faithful were ever so slowly gathering for the class. The Clerk of Session was a slim, erect man of about 70 whom everyone called Mr. Harry. I never saw him dressed any way other than impeccably, in a tailored business suit which I always imagined was a recent change for him from a frock coat, cravat, and spats. He gingerly approached Mrs. Hannah carrying a small bucket: "Here you are," he said as he put one hand on her shoulder with a wry little smile, "Some cleaning supplies. One of the chairs was sticky this morning and we would appreciate it if you could clean them for us after your children are out."

Her body literally jolting with the blow of what he said, Mrs. Hannah looked at him through her thick glasses, blinking and staring for a moment that seemed like an hour, then she broke down in a flood of tears. Instead of the bread of thanks for the relationships she was building, she had been handed once again the perpetual stone to remind her that the Saturday kids were, at best, a nuisance, and that, to the church leadership, sticky chairs were a big deal, neighborhood children were not. My hackles were raised, and I got involved in what became a Sunday morning rhubarb with Mr. Harry and the church elders: a true us *vs.* them, new *vs.* old confrontation in support of what I saw as one woman's determination to hold up a flickering light of promise in what was otherwise a mausoleum passing as a house of faith.

Come Monday morning the elders denounced me to the Presbytery and I was ordered out the church, effective immediately. Mrs. Hannah and I appealed their decision; we went to see the Presbytery bigwig himself, whose name I've not surprisingly forgotten, in his downtown office. We sat waiting for him for a good part of the morning, and when he finally came out he informed us that it was lunch time and we would have to come back later in the afternoon. We never had our meeting, but I was introduced to the fine ecclesiastical practice of *faux*-polite stonewalling. The whole experience was my rude awakening to the seamy side of religious politics which abjures clear and forthright dialogue in favor of an incense-filled back room. One thing that Mr. Harry said to me that morning, or rather shouted at me, was that, "I had better know" that in their ecclesiastical system there was no voice for a person like me who was neither a member, officer, nor minister. Without consciously realizing it, I had concluded somewhere inside me, then and there, that I would go to seminary and get ordained as a teaching elder just to have credentials to be able to have my say with all the *Mr. Harrys* of this world.

I never went back to the church, but Mrs. Hannah and I stayed in touch until she died. The church expired before she did, though, having lived on like Methuselah for years beyond what even imagination could bear. I was, and will always remain puzzled that no one ever wanted to talk at any level, and that no one beside Mrs. Hannah and her helpers ever thought much of the gift of new life that she struggled with all her soul to bring. But I always wondered how blissful it might have been if Mr. Harry or the Elders had appeared just once on a Saturday night and learned the names, if nothing else the names, of the young people, their neighbors, who were having the time of their lives singing and laughing away and making the sacred walls of their beloved Evangel Church shake with happiness and life.

WITH THE INHERITED IDEALISM of the *Risorgimento* flowing in my veins, I was beginning to dream of organizing a community around a simple ideal: a place where homeless and housed could meet together at the same table, giving, as each had to give, of themselves in service to each other. Too lofty, perhaps, or maybe too simple to be meaningful, but the formation of everything in my life thus far had taken me to that place. Frankly, I didn't even know if anyone else would think it was an idea worth pursuing; that is until the glorious summer of 1971 when I had the life-changing good fortune of meeting Marsha Young at Nyack College in Nyack, New York. She had experienced her own itinerant childhood as the daughter of a career army officer who was moved, with his family, every other year from pillar to post around the country and the world. My friendship with Marsha, a fellow outsider and my partner in life for 35 years, led to a commitment to work together in the project that we came to call Meeting Ground. I felt the best path to put a foundation under the dream was through the church, mustering the energy of persons like the ones I had come to know when I was going through my chaotic adolescence. I enrolled in Princeton Seminary in 1975 and three years later was ordained a Presbyterian minister. After an early start as pastor of a small, yet loving church, Christ Presbyterian in Springfield, Massachusetts, Marsha and I decided it was time to pull up stakes and pursue the vision.

We were drawn to Maryland through an intuition I had in 1976 while at a retreat on the Chesapeake Bay. I arrived early and found myself virtually alone there. Just at sunset at the end of a perfect autumn day, I set about to investigate the site, Camp Tockwogh, a rustic YMCA center on Maryland's Eastern Shore, named for the tribe of Native Americans who lived in the region. As I followed a trail through the woods, I came to a clearing at the Bay's edge, illuminated in bright moonlight, which ended at a sheer cliff dropping off sharply about a hundred feet into the water. It was a crisp, wild evening, pleasantly cool, and the swirling wind put everything around me in motion. As it grew darker, I found myself sitting on a large rock alone in a secluded niche of bushes, overlooking the turbulent waters. The gray, churning waves were like the soul of adventure, and I couldn't escape a growing sensation of presence. In this deepening experience, as night continued to fall, I felt I was not alone. At first it was eerie and exciting, then uplifting. In the early hours of the morning, I came away with a deep inner assurance that I was connected to the world and to all its life, and for no other reason than that within me, I knew that, for that brief moment at least, I had touched heaven. There was a profound certainty in it, and the memory of it drew me back to the shores of that great shellfish estuary where we planted the seeds for Meeting Ground, the community in which we labored for three decades in the pursuit of that ideal.

WHEN MY GRANDPARENTS FIRST stepped foot in America, it surely was a rare awakening: how far to come from an old country to one so gleaming new. They didn't arrive so much as they were reborn. They were surrounded by another world with new and unfamiliar relationships. Gone were the accustomed faces, hearths, and traditions which had been set for ages. Now, around another language and an unfamiliar Puritan heritage, even their time-honored, all-encompassing religion was alien company. In my family at least they struggled long, hard and unsuccessfully to find footing for their souls, and finding none, they bequeathed to me the uncompleted quest to unearth at last the place we call home.

Meeting Ground

Dear Mom, I am a boy. When I grow up I will get money. I will buy you a house. Love, Quentin

NOTE TO A HOMELESS MOTHER FROM HER 6-YEAR-OLD SON

It would be impossible to describe in a single chapter all that Meeting Ground was and is. That story, including the multitude of remarkable people who are part of it, and to whom I owe a debt I can never hope to repay, is a book in itself, and that may come someday. What I can offer here is an introduction, a setting for many of the stories that follow. It's just the bare bones of a stunning narrative of three decades in which my life has been educated and enthralled by my relationships with ordinary people in some extraordinary circumstances.

We launched Meeting Ground in 1982 and our decision as to where to begin was confirmed by a tree. It was tall and old with branches that spread out broadly to provide lots of summer shade. It stood right next to the front door of what was to become Wayfarers' House in Elkton, Maryland. The building was a nine bedroom Victorian-style residence, once the home of a minister who performed weddings in this former elopement capital of the East Coast. On our first visit, the owner stopped me as we were coming down the front steps. Pointing up to the stately oak he asked, "What do you think of the tree?" His question, seemingly from out of nowhere, astonished me since we were attracted to the house because it was the tree we had first noticed. "I thought it might have something to do with your interest in the house," he went on to say, further arousing my surprise. Had we done or said anything to make him ask that? We were sure we hadn't, but his seeming awareness of its importance to us only stoked our curiosity about the house.

Months before, when the idea of Meeting Ground was taking shape in my mind, the image of a tree appeared with it. An artist friend sketched what I had visualized, and it became the logo for the cause. It seemed appropriate. A tree is ancient representation of spiritual connection, a bridge between earth and sky; it symbolized the ideal we wanted to make real. Meeting Ground was all in the mind then, until I first saw that tree in front of the house for sale on Delaware Avenue. It was, strikingly, just like the aspiration on paper. It was the tree that drew us seriously to consider what we otherwise might have ignored as a blunderbuss of a building, too tired and needing repair to serve our needs. The tree was the sign. We never fully understood why that was, but we cashed out our savings, got the building and launched *Wayfarers' House.*

Marsha and I and our three-year-old daughter Alessandra moved into it on May 25, 1982. With the help of lots of volunteers, we began right away to get the place ready, but even before we were half-finished homeless people began coming for help, desperately seeking shelter. A young man named Tony was the first to arrive, brought by a woman from a church in New Jersey. She had heard about what we were doing and thought it would be a match for someone without a family who needed a base to get a start in life. He was followed within a few days by an extended family—eight children, mother Mary, father Joseph [yes, the names are correct] and *Pops*, the grandfather. They were followed within a short time by several other single adults mostly young, mostly alienated from their families. The house filled up overnight it seemed, and our hands were full in the same order.

The beginning ideal of Meeting Ground, as I have said, was a simple one: a table, a powerful symbol of one-ness, around which all would be welcome, and there rich and poor, homeless and housed, could meet together. It was set especially for persons who were experiencing homelessness, something I knew about all too well, but it was meant for anyone. A benign idea, I thought at first, who wouldn't welcome it? But I learned early on that talking about unconditional hospitality was one thing, say from the pulpit where it could be overlooked or accepted as a wistful notion, but it was another thing to do it—*not in our back yard.* The public hearing for a permit to open Wayfarers' House was ugly. A vocal and hostile zoning board, stimulated and egged-on by an irate audience of potential neighbors, questioned us for hours on everything from personal finances to our *real motives,* and would we not be just a vile gathering of motorcyclists, tramps, criminals and, most suspicious of all, other do-gooders? Those organized against it were not what we expected; most were prominent parishioners from local churches. I learned then, and through countless similar trials, that all an ordained minister needs to do to burst the aura of polite and deferential respectability is to try putting unconditional hospitality into practice. But we also learned that idealism attracts talented comrades. A young lawyer I had never met before, Dennis Clower, came forward, took up our cause, and fought forcefully at that hearing and many others in years following. He was a passionate advocate, even to the point of bringing some of the mocking criticism on himself.

The zoning board flatly rejected our application for an occupancy permit on the ground that [believe this] it was unlawful to practice a religion in a residential zone. We took our case to Circuit Court where Judge Thomas Cole, reading glasses on the end of his nose, leaning back on his chair while flipping through papers, and slowly ruminating out loud about the case in a kind of plodding undercurrent, finally determined that, since the area was approved for boarding houses all we needed do was to start charging folks a dime-a-month rent and we'd be legal. Just like that. It turned out that our strongest asset in the struggle was sincere persistence—of course with some faith in the ultimate triumph of goodwill and the help of one slightly bewildered judge. I always think if it hadn't worked out the way it did, we would have started anyway. Sometimes it's better to be a little naïve, and not back off when others declare the road closed. Not knowing ahead of time that something can't be done, not being bound to following the orthodox plan for how things should be done, can lead sometimes to the surprise of achieving the impossible.

From the beginning many committed folks like Dennis came to help and, in a spirit of sacrifice, share the burden and make the project happen. But not all who came understood what Meeting Ground was about; many especially missed the meaning of the table. A middle-aged woman, who prided herself as a peacemaker and supporter of liberal causes, came to explore how she might help as a volunteer. She arrived midmorning, and as we walked through Wayfarers' House she noticed a pile of unwashed plates in the sink. "Oh!" She reacted with a noticeable start, "Don't they wash their breakfast dishes?" She had said a lot in those six words. The meaning of the table is to blur the societal line between *us* and *them* and to say that *we* sit together, and at the table we reject judgment based on any label or stereotype. Perhaps her typecast was that whoever would live at a place like Wayfarers' House, homeless or otherwise, would be lazy or irresponsible. Maybe washing the breakfast dishes before the toast is cold is a sign of higher social class or personal industry? When, as a volunteer, she would actually meet and get to know others, she might then use a disorderly sink as an opportunity to gather a group to wash and dry together with her, easing the anxiety by taking the better part.

WILLETT (BILL) SMITH, A PRESBYTERIAN minister, was one of the persons most influential in the beginning of Meeting Ground. He was pastor of Limestone Church in Wilmington, Delaware. If there is such a thing as serendipity, encountering Bill was it for me. He picked me to do my seminary fieldwork at his church, probably because no one else had applied that year. The first time I heard him preach, I realized he was granting as much credence to the writings of Martin Buber, Henry David Thoreau, Abraham Joshua Heschel, and Frederick Denison Maurice as to the Bible itself. And listening to his sermons was as refreshing as ice water in the desert. He didn't follow the usual rules: he could ramble, and his eye contact was spotty, but he lifted everyone with his humor and whatever he said you knew he believed with all his heart. When I first approached him with the idea of Meeting Ground his response was, "Sounds like a good idea, but I think you're going to lose your shirt." That comment I never let him forget.

He was a mentor who became a friend to me and to Meeting Ground in the early days when we needed all the encouragement we could get. He heightened my thinking to see that a person could be outside institutional religion and still be part of the church. When he thought some bureaucratic ecclesiastical process violated the human spirit or offended the *I-thou*, he would forcefully object, and he was never inclined to be tactful. As part of the Greatest Generation, he fought in of the Battle of the Bulge during World War II, and it stirred a deep compassion in him. After that, he once told me, he was never inclined to serve ideology before empathy or basic human kindness.

Bill's philosophy was summarized by what Dorothy Day used to call *personalism*: a person mattered more than a thing, even if that *thing* was a sacred book. He always thought the Jewish philosopher Martin Buber said it best: that a human relationship should never be an *I-it*, as one to an object, but always *I-Thou*, as one to a beloved. In Thoreau, he discovered the fierce importance of knowing who we are as a person so we could be genuine in our association with others. In the social activism of Maurice and the moral pragmatism of Heschel, he taught that our true religion was, simply, the quality of our affection for people. *Love thy neighbor* was to Bill not merely a wishful ideal, but a moral imperative never to lose faith in anyone. He always gave me hope because, while he worked through ecclesiastical institutions, he was quick to see how the *letter of the law* could harm rather than heal, and that holiness was not in the rigor of rules, but in the rightness of relationships. He once helped make a video about Meeting Ground, expressing in it the ideals of the community about as well as anyone ever did:

> *People don't want just to be fed; they want to be befriended. People who are in trouble don't always want a handout or a peanut butter sandwich, they want to meet someone; to experience human affection and concern, and they want to be befriended in the good and healthy sense of befriending: met and embraced. [These meetings] draw you into something that's open ended, and*

scary only in the sense it's going to challenge some very old stereotypes you have and you're going to have to abandon some very old opinions you've held–if you want the meetings to take place. I highly recommend it if you want to become your true self. I think it's a good place to begin.

SHORTLY AFTER WE BEGAN Meeting Ground, a young graduate student from Middle Tennessee State University, born and raised poor in Appalachia, came to volunteer for the summer. Terry was unusually gifted in relating to other people, apt to be playful with anyone, from a quick game of catch with a depressed senior before supper, to corralling a couple of teenagers to help her pick up donated supplies. Even after three decades I can still see her slowly walking in the back yard with a full tool belt swaying around her waist, taking measured steps, engrossed in listening to the troubles of a newly arrived homeless woman. She had learned the art of empathy the hard way as a child. Her home life was as broken down as the house she lived in. Her father was a hard drinker, mercifully not around much, while her mother struggled alone to eke out their hardscrabble living. Life was tough and hope-deprived, but Terry, young and unjaded by it all, believed in herself and in her capacity to grow stronger.

Things changed for her dramatically one early morning at the age of fourteen, while she was still sleeping. Without a knock, the door of her bedroom opened and a group of adults, unknown to her, walked right in. They were church volunteers who had come to fix up the dilapidated house. Barely acknowledging her presence, they proceeded among themselves to measure and plan how they would be doing her room, even down to the color of the paint. As suddenly as they had come, they left, and she was alone with a profound emptiness, feeling that strangers, albeit well-meaning, had entered her life uninvited and, by not even asking her opinion, robbed her of something sacred. She felt like a piece of furniture that morning. In their charitable intent, they had, unwittingly but without flinching, crushed her budding spirit. Had they only met her first and come to know her as a person and asked her permission and advice—or even more, offered to help her to remodel her own room in her own house—it would have been a world of difference. For a long time she felt like she was in a deep dark well with a wound that wouldn't heal. She eventually found her way out of the pit and back into the sunlight in a step-by-step climb by recruiting her own group of volunteers to help others in the way she had wished others had helped her: by meeting and including.

BEFORE WE BARELY HAD GOTTEN started at Wayfarers' House it was clear we needed more space, especially for homeless families. The old house was filled to the gills with people of every kind, smiling heads popping out all the windows like the old woman who lived in the shoe. We were considering all kinds of possibilities, but it was finally a little girl and a puppy-sized, lop-eared hare that gave us the idea for Clairvaux Farm. It happened one day when a new family arrived, a mother with her newborn baby and three-year-old daughter. They were driven over by their social worker in a state-owned four-door sedan. The adults stepped out, the young mother cradling her baby with one arm and the other reaching inside the back seat for the hand of her daughter, but the little girl would not budge from the car. Her mother tugged relentlessly; the social worker stepped in to give an assist from the other door, but the girl resisted all the more, firmly clutching anything she could grasp, using arms and legs like an unfolding umbrella and holding on for dear life. We all knew what was happening but were powerless to make a difference. The girl was terrified of one more bag-and-baggage move to yet another strange place on top of, only God knows, how many others she had already endured. She was not coming out of the car.

Until, that is, one of the children living in the house got an idea. He and several others had been standing nearby watching when he suddenly, out of the blue, ran to the back yard. Opening a cage, he scooped up one of the large hares we were keeping as pets. We were all surprised, dazzled really, when he stepped out from behind the house, clutching the big furry bundle tightly with both hands against his chest. He came over to the car, the social worker stepped away, and he stood up close to the open door, holding the rabbit in two hands offering the ungainly bundle of fur, long ears, twitching nose and worried eyes to the frightened girl. We watched with astonishment as she instantly relaxed, smiled, and scrambled out of the car to hug it—happily giggling, she and the boy together. Had we not seen it with our eyes, we might not have believed it. We went from an impossible situation to something like a miracle—but actually just the common sense of a boy who, lacking all the learned wisdom of we adults, rightly reasoned with his heart. It was one of those rare times when the beauty of beholding sucks the air out of everything else and all we could do was stand by and watch, formerly wise mouths struck dumb. The futility of all our former efforts was unmasked by the summary of these young hearts, speaking without words to each other, in their innocence unaware of the sheer splendor of the moment.

Life lessons come in many sizes, and this one was about a small girl's imagination of home. What trained professionals and even a loving mother could not accomplish, an unwitting fellow creature and a quick thinking child achieved easily. Brooke seized the opportunity to soothe the fright she saw in the eyes of a decidedly nervous bunny, and by holding another, she was able to let go of her own immobilizing terror and take a step forward in her life.

In that encounter, a prophet-like summons to stay close to zeal of our first love, we found our new direction. Our next step forward would be to locate a farm, a country place where homeless children would know the minute they arrived that this move would be different. We wanted a place where the lessons of rabbits could be learned. In the summer of 1983, we found a 20 acre property for sale in Earleville, Maryland near the Bay and not far from Elkton, and we went for it. It was half woods and pasture, half ravine and marsh. On the high ground there was a century-old paint-peeling farmhouse and two ailing barns, but it was all grass and trees as far as the eye could see. Miraculously, within a month, we raised the down payment, secured the financing, and on October 1 we, along with three homeless families, spent our first night at the place we named Clairvaux Farm, honoring the great 11th century Saint Bernard whose religious practice turned much of Europe into a shelter for the dispossessed.

   WITHIN DAYS AFTER WE OPENED Wayfarers' House, and before we got the farm, a volunteer bringing donations, backing his car without looking, slammed his rear bumper into our mystic tree, ripping off a huge piece of bark. He returned the next day to daub the bare trunk with pitch in the hope the tree would live, but it didn't work; within six months it was dead, and we cut it down. Saying we were sorry to see it go is more than an understatement, but in its demise the tree's story was even more a harbinger of things to come. As it had been a sign of our idealism, so losing it was a symbol of coming reality, as indeed it turned out that Meeting Ground became—like the course of life itself, a crucible of hope mixed with heartache. We, who had entered the adventure with such high spirit of promise, quickly found that the nitty-gritty sometimes killed the neat ideals right before our eyes, leaving us to despair or else recast our dreams. The latter has served us well over the years, mostly in finding that the ideals are not realized in the high hopes of marvelous things accomplished, but in sharing the strength and frailty of who we are, each of us meeting one another on the road to a place we least expected.

IDENTITY: Meeting Ourselves

Each of us is all the sums he has not counted: subtract us into nakedness and night again, and you shall see begin in Crete four thousand years ago the love that ended yesterday in Texas.

THOMAS WOLFE, *Look Homeward Angel*

EMIGRANT SHIP *ROMA*, 1902

A Future Rising

To cheat oneself out of love is the most terrible deception; it is an eternal loss for which there is no reparation, either in time or in eternity....Never cease loving a person, and never give up hope for her, for even the prodigal son who had fallen most low, could still be saved; the bitterest enemy and also he who was your friend could again be your friend; love that has grown cold can kindle again.

SOREN KIERKEGAARD

The urgency of detail

Growing up in the throes of insecurity taught me that homelessness creates in a person's life, especially in a child, a dysfunction of detail. On the whirligig of anxiety and disappointment, the struggle to survive, for even the best intentioned parents, can consume everything, and the little things, small yet vitally essential to a child, the things most people take for granted like regular meals, clean clothing, or even basic school supplies are ignored or just plumb forgotten. It may not be for lack of love on the part of the parents or other caregivers, but homelessness has a way of corroding the details, and as it happens repeatedly it sends message: you are not like the other children, yours is not the important life, the future will not rise for you as it will for them. As surely as a drippy faucet at night will rob our sleep, the ceaseless repetition of these small abandonments will gnaw the peace out of a child's soul.

Sometime around 1995 at Clairvaux Farm, I saw Selena standing alone on a cold morning outside the warm dining hall. The winter air was heavy with the chill, but it also carried the savory smells of coffee brewing and bacon frying. Folks were gathering for breakfast outside the door and beginning to come in.

This four-year-old girl was among them, but alone by herself waiting for her mother. In my rush to get inside and warm, and lured into a sense of urgency that often characterizes our behavior when it's focused on the most trivial, I walked right past without truly seeing her.

Just as my hand touched to the doorknob, she spoke, in words so soft I could have pretended not to hear: "Can you button my coat?" I couldn't open the door; there was a conversation in my head that went something like, "Maybe she's talking to somebody else, someone just standing around like she is, maybe it's not to me since I'm in a rush to breakfast..." It was all immensely unconvincing; I turned around and went to do as she asked—on this frigid morning her quiet plea was compelling and absolute.

Trying to cover up for my breakfast fixation, I put on an awkward repentant smile as I got down on one knee to button her coat. In that short moment, as I was only trying to do what she had asked, I unexpectedly entered into a complex relationship and a moment that stunned me. The coat had no buttons. She looked at me: her eyes were uncertain, doubtful, and asking, perhaps demanding, so much what she expressed through her buttons, or rather, her lack of buttons. In her face I saw myself, only a few years before, and I easily read the message in her expression.

Getting her a coat with buttons was the easy part; more difficult was to answer her real question, one calling for the honesty of an involvement in her life, to meet who she actually was. I suddenly understood that to her, something as small as the lack of a button was nothing less than the understanding of her place in the world, and, in its vastness, whether there was a true sentiment for her. Here and now, standing against the wind of loneliness, she had inquired about the possibility of love, and whether there was, indeed, an unconditional faith on anyone's part as to her value and place. When all is said and done, true religion may be less about concern with the function of cathedrals and more about the dysfunction of buttons.

It is said that religious people are a people of the book, and that the book is supposed to be inviolable. If that's true, her life also must be infallible. She is more sacred than any writing, because she is why the dreams of the book are spun in the first place. Until what's written becomes real for the Selenas of this world, it's just paper pressed wistfully to our chests. Life to life is how the book is read and maybe the future that is rising will bring us to our senses. There is no book. There is only us.

A Raw Man

... to lose the earth you know for greater knowing; to lose the life you have, for greater life; to leave the friends you loved, for greater loving; to find a land more kind than home, more large than earth.

THOMAS WOLFE, *You Can't Go Home Again*

Overcoming doughnuts

I first came to know William Asnis in 1986 at Friendship House, Meeting Ground's old thrift store turned homeless shelter on Market Street in Wilmington, Delaware. I had a camera and was taking pictures and Bill told me not to photograph him. "I've been told," he said, "No publicity!" That phrase, "No publicity," I soon learned was Bill's watchword. He relied on inner messages: voices he called angels which guided him somehow. He also saw beams of light shining on certain people, similar to auras, and what he called spirit beings. These apparitions were not vague presences, but real people; he would often name them: Saint Francis of Assisi and the celebrated contralto Marian Anderson are among many of the personalities that Bill said inhabited the old store. Occasionally, while he was talking with me, he would shift his eyes as if he were looking rather seriously at somebody or something right behind the side of my head: as a person would do if they suddenly noticed a bug crawling in my hair. I'd learned to take it in stride; it was usually just a glance and he'd be back to making eye contact and talking. Yet, I always wondered who or what had caught his attention, but was always a bit too afraid to ask.

Bill was admired, even revered, by other street people who respectfully nicknamed him *Praying Bill*. He lived without using any money, which he considered evil, and survived living on the street and by whatever temporary comfort he might find in shelters and soup kitchens. Describing himself as an ex-college professor and ex-minister turned pilgrim, he was a graduate of Cornell who was a rising star at the University of California-Santa Cruz, where he taught creative writing. He made a sudden decision to leave it all in a Saint-Francis-like worldly renunciation and, in the mode of a wandering Russian *Starets,* he slowly migrated east eventually taking up residence on the streets of Wilmington. When I first met him there, he was tall and lanky, almost gaunt, with unkempt hair and beard, ragged in appearance. His dark eyes were firm, and their contact direct, deep, and constant, except when he was listening to his inner voice, and they would turn inward like he were looking inside himself.

On the streets, Bill was universally loved, but he could easily be dismissed by those who didn't know him as just another minor human failure, aimlessly drifting among other misfits. But to walk with Bill on the city sidewalks could be a time of rare inspiration. He described a reality vastly different from the everyday life of most people. Beyond the illusion, corruption, and deadly seriousness of the world of politics and money, he saw a living presence, working steadily in and around everyone, patiently bringing all people into what he called rightness. Considering mass media a form of corruption which fed on negativity, he ignored the diversions of newspapers, television and the like while passionately exhorting each person he met to believe in the possibility of change, no matter how dire their situation. Hoping to give him some relief from a rough existence, I once got him to leave the city and stay at my house overnight. I talked with him for a while before turning in, and left him sitting in a kind of meditation. In the morning, I found him still sitting in the same spot on an unruffled bed; he couldn't sleep because it was "too comfortable," and he leaned on me to get him back to the streets right away so he could "get some rest."

People always asked, and I often wondered myself, why such a thoughtful, deeply motivated person would choose to live such an ascetic life, indeed much like a 20th Century St. Francis? Many regretfully disregarded him as mentally ill, but Bill could not so casually be brushed away; he had a quiet, intelligent resonance.

I was always certain that Bill chose to live on the streets more to know God than to know about God, even as he lived in homeless poverty for love of persons in the same circumstance. Their despair was not in Bill's imagination; it was part of his life also, and just as his knowledge of God was rooted in life's reality, so was his knowledge of people.

He described the Old Testament Prophets, like Isaiah and Jeremiah, as raw people—those who live passionately to know themselves and others. They are persons who revere the eternal; they are *raw* because they are truthful and always alive to the possibility of new love. Their world is broad, as is their prophetic view, which until the end of time calls us back to our common purpose in life. Once when we were standing together in a soup kitchen line waiting to be served, Bill broke a long silence by quietly saying to me, "Someday we will overcome these doughnuts." Seeing my puzzled reaction he continued, "Learning to serve doughnuts is easier for most people than learning to serve God. There may come a day when the people now standing in line will be served a portion of God instead of a doughnut." I wondered aloud, "Will anyone still want to come to breakfast without the doughnuts?" "You might be surprised," he responded. Love, he determined, is not so much a charitable act as it is a willingness, even eagerness, to know another person and to share their life, however briefly.

We once had to keep an extremely sick homeless man in the back room of the thrift store. He had been brought to us by other homeless men who were adamant that he was too ill to be on the streets. Bill immediately took it upon himself to stay with him, and he rarely left his side in the two weeks he was with us. Their two lives became abundantly intertwined as he slept next to him, prepared his meals, and kept him from being alone. All the while Bill patiently taught us, in the back room of a dilapidated storefront, what he meant when he admonished us to *serve God to others*.

A dictionary might define virtue as: *moral excellence, goodness, conformity of life and conduct to moral laws, uprightness, and rectitude.* But virtue is also that which is necessary for humanity's far reaching vision: the long view for insight into destination and destiny, always asking what kind of beings we are and where we, as a people, are headed. As he daily walked the streets of Wilmington, Bill was sure always to keep one foot rooted on the ageless shore of heaven, which he knew surrounded him on earth, and he wanted everyone to see what he saw so vividly. Praying Bill died in 2005 on the streets where he had lived so long. He was a raw person, an unshakable instrument of peace, and always so consistently and unrelentingly hopeful that we all might so be.

What Makes Us Who We Are

One thing we know, which the white man may one day discover. Our God is the same God. You may think now that you own God as you wish to own our land. But you cannot. God is the Body of humankind. And God's compassion is equal for the red man and the white.

CHIEF SEALTH, OF THE DUWAMISH TRIBE OF THE STATE OF WASHINGTON
*Written in 1855 to President Franklin Pierce concerning
the proposed purchase of the tribe's land*

Buoyant weakness

One winter's night in 2007, fifty of us were in the fellowship room of a church which was serving for the night as an emergency shelter. Thirty-five were homeless children and adults for whom there was no other place to go, and the rest were volunteers. As was our custom, everyone had formed a circle for grace before supper, and the leader asked for a volunteer to say it. An eleven-year-old girl, homeless with her family, quickly raised her hand, waving it, eager to pray, and we, like a chorus of wilting daffodils, assumed the position in unison of lowering heads, closing eyes, and wondering how long the grace would take before we could eat. I had expected her, as a child, to be at least a little intimidated in this group of adults, to say her prayer softly and quietly. Instead, she defied all expectation: speaking clearly, vibrantly, with a voice of gentle confidence, not in church-words but in most sincere heart: *"Thanks, God that we have a place to sleep and food, and for the nice people here, and that's about all I can think of..."* She paused for half a minute and then said, *"Well, I'll say goodbye for now, but I'll be talking to you later before I go to sleep. Amen."*

It was the earnest and warm prayer of a young girl who conversed with God as if it were the self-same hand she held in hers. We were a half dozen different churches represented in that circle, including some strong theological contrasts, even some with no religious belief at all, but as we slowly, one by one, looked up from her prayer there were few dry eyes. This child had taken us by the hand to another place, as we furtively, sheepishly caught each other's glance, slightly embarrassed that we had been so suddenly transported there, an inkling of heaven within and among ourselves.

In a split instant, we entered a gleaming new commonality: we were no longer what we had been just seconds before. We experienced our individual selves, and each other, in the vulnerability of what it is to be human, and if only for a brief moment, understood our unity, not through common opinion, but through the fragile and tender nature that we share together–so powerful in its claim on our hearts and so infinite in its possibility to turn our predictable little world upside down.

An Old Woman's Parting Legacy

Signs happen to us without respite; living means being addressed, we would only need present ourselves and to perceive.... Each of us is encased in an armor which we soon, out of familiarity, cease to notice. There are only moments which penetrate it and stir the soul to sensibility.

MARTIN BUBER

Ultimate good

As a college student in the 1960's, I spent my summers working in New York City, in a small, but mighty, Episcopal mission on Manhattan's lower west side, in the neighborhood ominously known as Hell's Kitchen. The community was crowded and diverse—Puerto Rican, African, Italian, Eastern and Western European, even a family of native Alaskans—and, it seemed, just as many religions, everything from Jehovah's Witness to Roman Catholic to the *Iglesia Pentecostal*. There were single adults efficiently rooming alone, street people, and families in old brownstone tenements.

The mission itself was in one of these 3-story brownstones, built sometime in the late 19th century, in the middle of a block of ethnic restaurants, apartment buildings, and cheap hotels. It was mildly famous in the city because of its 12-foot-high neon-lit cross, which continually flashed, *Sin Will Find You Out* on one side and *Get Right With God* on the other. That little refuge of English Victorian religion, with its staff of dedicated lifers and summer volunteers, tried to have something for everybody: from youth gatherings to funeral services it was in every respect the neighborhood church; homeless and housed alike sat together at the same table in that place, for meals as for worship services.

I loved getting to know the people who lived in the neighborhood, and when I was intensely active in that little world the pain of the bigger world of politics and war appeared surreal and irrelevant. The escalating conflict in Vietnam, along with all the cultural turbulence of that era, seemed so far away to me during the summer. The real problems were what happened to the kids we lost for several hours at the World's Fair in Queens, or how to get a shower for old Stanley who lived in a rain-sodden upholstered chair on the street. Daily my world-view was revolutionized by the people I knew and the things I learned, and never more so than late one hot New York night as I walked with a friend, Mary Vaught, a retired missionary to Lebanon, on an unusually dark West 51st Street on our way back to the mission.

As we passed a sunken doorway, we were stopped and curiously drawn by what sounded like a low moan. Looking down we saw a pile of rags and cardboard, not rubbish but a distinctly human nest, and in the pile, barely distinguishable from the trash, was a person. She was an old woman, dreadfully frail, sick and too weak to move; her long groans requiring all her effort. The unexpected scene stunned us into a kind of paralysis: trying to grasp what we were actually seeing and at the same time our thoughts racing as to what to do.

There was little choice. We spoke to her, gently picked her up, and carried what was a featherlight bundle in our arms back to the mission. We fixed her on a cot and called for an ambulance which took her to Bellevue hospital. The next day I went to visit her there.

Sitting by her bed was painful and uplifting at the same time. She looked so old, thin and tired, but she had been washed now and was on clean sheets. Her wrinkled skin was thick and grey, her whole body with only slightly more substance than her soul, so light it could seem, at the slightest beckon, to float. She smiled, but it was a melancholy expression, as if she were looking past me at something or someone far away. She tried to speak, but there were no words, only sounds as though she were going in and out of life. I couldn't tell if she even knew I was there, but that didn't seem to matter. I kept vigil as long as I could, and left her again in the kind care of strangers; when I returned to visit the next day, her bed was empty.

I am still, after half a century, moved with rugged emotion when I recall her. Who was she? Someone's much beloved daughter, sister, mother, or wife? And why was she finally in such mean circumstances, so alone and friendless? I was, perhaps, the last relationship in her life, if it could be called that, and I never even knew her name, nor she mine as far as I could tell. I was young, just starting life, and I held the hand of someone I never knew as she was ending hers. As I sat by her bed in what proved to be her last moments, I felt something akin to worship; how a person feels when lifted to an inexpressible oneness, a harmony with all that is; from a fortune of circumstance our lives had more than crossed: they mixed, as if intertwined, that in the moment of her life's final loneliness, neither of us should be alone.

Over the years, this meeting has not dimmed in my memory. I think about it often, and how it changed me. What she gave me, as a parting legacy, was the sentience of awe, that discomforting mystery at the edges of all life. Though we appeared to be worlds apart in who we were, the old woman and the young man were somehow not different in any respect that mattered: she and I were one and the same person. As implausible as it may sound, there is no other way to explain the bond of our common source. Much as we would divide the world into *us and them*, there is only *we*, or, in fact, more like *one*: in where we have come from and in who we are.

Like anyone else, I have my moments, actually most of the time, when I want to distance myself from my more alien-species, stranger-than-life cousins, and society does more resemble the Hatfields and McCoys than Tristan and Iseult, but maybe that's the fantastic stuff of the dream from which we hope to awaken.

Our common origin and the deeper meaning of our relationships reveals itself in moments when, still half asleep, we may suddenly be aroused for a living moment by those grand fortunes of circumstance to open our eyes and see things as they actually are. This ever attending benevolence may defy explanation, but it is not subtle: it surrounds us; at any moment it may bring us back to ourselves. It is a goodness that is not bound by any creed or limitation of thought. It is ever reaching, ever desiring, ever calling us home to who we are: it is the ultimate good. The name *God* is simply a contraction of the old English word *good*. That is so apt. God is good. Perhaps it is just that simple.

Slim Odds

In a thicket at the foot of the Himalayan Mountains there once lived a parrot together with many other animals and birds. One day a fire started in the thicket from the friction of bamboos in a strong wind and the birds and animals were in frightened confusion. The parrot, feeling compassion for their fright and suffering and wishing to repay the kindness he had received in the bamboo thicket where he could shelter himself, tried to do all he could to save them. He dipped himself in a pond nearby and flew over the fire and shook off the drops of water to extinguish the fire. He repeated this diligently with a heart of compassion out of gratitude to the thicket.

This spirit of kindness and self-sacrifice was noticed by a heavenly god who came down from the sky and said to the parrot: "You have a gallant mind, but what good do you expect to accomplish by a few drops of water against this great fire?" The parrot answered: "There is nothing that cannot be accomplished by the gallant spirit of gratitude within me. I will try over and over again and then over in the next life." The great god was impressed by the parrot's spirit and together they extinguished the fire.

A BUDDHIST STORY

The tree of life

On a summer night around 1993, during a violent thunderstorm, a lightning bolt scored a direct hit on a lone elm tree standing proudly at our Clairvaux Farm entrance lane. The jolt was so severe that it blew a large hole in the trunk and started the tree on fire. Persons in the farmhouse who had literally been shaken out of bed by the thunder gazed out the windows in amazement as flames roared from the tree's heart. All the next day we watched smoke streaming from a gash in the trunk , until, by evening, it had all settled into embers which continued to glow from deep inside the tree's gutted body, slowly consuming everything it could until the once proud elm stood hollow from its roots up through its trunk. It is now many years later, and the old tree continues to bloom, as it has every spring since, and that's the real story: not the tree's demise, but its incredible endurance.

The lesson in this may seem transparent: like the tree, we are inspired to stand as tall and confident so that we too can survive even the most violent of life's challenges. Resisting the adversity of fate which, like a playful Greek god capriciously tossing lightning bolts into our unsuspecting lives, we fight to stand erect through the bedlam of senseless catastrophe.

Yet the tale of the stricken tree goes deeper. Something even more deadly struck after the lightning had gone and the sky was again calm. While it had heroically survived fire, it now had to stand alone and listen to bystander humans discuss how it "needed to be cut down," It was essentially dead, many commented, "a goner," and should be eliminated before it either "fell on somebody or else slowly rotted as an insect attracting eyesore right at the Farm's front door." Our beautiful tree had endured the lightning, but could it now survive the pounding negativity of its critics who were not at all convinced that it had what it took to function after such a disaster?

A few weeks after this happened, I was attending a housing conference in Dover, Delaware. Lunch was a buffet, and the line was long, so I decided to get some fresh air in the courtyard and wait outside. I was pleasantly surprised to see an old friend there, someone I would never have expected to see at this event, who also had the same idea about the lunch line, and we soon were engrossed in conversation. Tracey had been homeless as a child and young teenager and was now in her early 20's. In her younger years, she had been struck by something like lightning, and the bolt was far more powerful than that which got the tree. It was of the sort that strikes the vulnerable, tender heart and soul of an innocent, and she had only recently emerged from the smoldering embers of many years of catastrophic homelessness, with its inherent abuse and neglect. Her sheer survival was due to that wondrous life-force which has the power to carry us even through fire, but she had done much more than that. When she came of age, she made a new home for herself and her younger brother and sister, and she now has children of her own and works hard as a nurse as she continues to further her education. As we spoke that afternoon, I was captivated by her growing and large vision of the world and of life itself. She couldn't be satisfied just to survive, even given the enormity of that accomplishment in itself. She wanted to achieve, to aspire to a greater goal of service to others, and her face was alive with hope and energy. All the while we talked, I wondered: how has she come to this place in her life after all she has endured?

Even more persuasive was her life impulse which had prevailed against the forces of bitterness, negativity, and heartbreak. She too had her share of bystanders who never thought she would blossom again, like the tree, so full of renewed life. The exceptional loneliness of her struggle against such odds, and that she had so emerged from years of chaos and sadness, is a mighty clue to the nature of our being, of who we are. Tracey's comment at the end of our conversation was stunning: "I have seen so much beauty in my life," she said, "I believe in that; my experience of the terrible things is the advantage I have of knowing what it's like, how it feels, and being able to really help other people who are going through what I've been through." Lightning may have struck her branches, but cradled deep within was strength which even a fire storm of negativity could not destroy. From this source, the water of her being was slowly taken up to restore and nourish what had been so capriciously and inexcusably harmed.

Such renewed life stands tall simply because of what it is. Like the battered tree, it sends a message that we can be made more beautiful and resilient in the struggle; that the patience of the life-force is inexhaustible. Something in us has the power to return like spring after winter, renewing our imagination and melting barriers that used to stand between ourselves and others. We know this because as we quietly stand and look into the heart of a hollow, gutted tree—it speaks to us. Incredibly, it beams to our marrow the dignity of creation: that the love of life is at our core and is not easily dissolved. This passion overcomes especially when the odds are slim in its favor, drawing strength even from the negativity which surrounds it. And anyone who doubts, needs to see this tree.

Call Me by My True Names

Please call me by my true names,
so I can hear all my cries and laughs at once,
so I can see that my joy and pain are one.
Please call me by my true names,
so I can wake up,
and so the door of my heart can be left open,
the door of compassion.

THICH NHAT HANH

Singular reality

Reality is sometimes a puzzling affair, especially when we are surrounded more by illusion than substance. When we drift too far from it, we can get the impression we are on another planet, a place so unfamiliar that we are desperate to return home, to the land within us, to ourselves. Sifting truth from lie is a lot like inspecting a well-made silk flower to tell if it's real or not: the one without flaws is the imitation. It's the absence of a faded brown leaf or discoloration of a petal that tips us off, so that eventually the living one will declare itself to us: heart to heart, because it's not perfect. Maybe that's why fantasy is so attractive: there's nothing to go wrong.

Sitting at a desk sorting through the mail is usually the most routine and uninspiring of jobs, but not on the day when I opened an envelope from Anna, an old friend of our community. In it was a handwritten letter and a carefully folded five dollar bill. The money dropped on the desk and lay there as I read the words of the note. It was from a women who had lived with us a year or two earlier, around 1990, and had stayed in touch ever since. Anna had tasted homelessness at every stage of her life; she grew up far from perfect. As with so many other children born to parents disturbed and distracted, she had it tough from the beginning; the neglect was not simply emotional and mental, it was also acutely physical. It scarred her for life: her health, ability to work, and her appearance to the world. With the odds against her, Anna could easily have given up, but she never did. Although her life was marked by days, months, and years of almost overwhelming struggle, she managed to find resources for living and to cope with each new challenge. Her faith in Anna was strong. It prospered her through a life which could easily have been stymied by hardship and sadness.

Although she lived in our community during the years she was experiencing homelessness, she never gave up on living independently. She may have had few physical and social resources available to her, but her soul was tempered with grace from a source within her. She was close to the age when most people retire when she felt lucky to land a subsistence-level job as caretaker for a bedridden patient in exchange for room and board. In that large house she claimed a small space as her new home, and there she kept her independence by helping another person through their own tough time.

As I quietly read the words of the note, "Please use this money to help the homeless," my own spirit lifted. On one side of reality, there was a mere five dollar bill on the table. What is so little when the monthly bills of our community are in the many thousands? Yet, on the other side, there is the marrow of life itself, and it is powerful in its presentation. Through all its flaws, shortcomings, weaknesses, and evils there is the dazzling reverberation that life communicates with life to affirm the unbounded generosity which underlies our relationships and speaks of the truth through which we are joined.

Anna's expression was a sacrifice, I knew that: five dollars was a significant part of the little she had, like the widow's mite she spoke through it of her identification with all who are adrift on this planet, all struggling at the edge of unsurpassed affluence to scrape together, with a small bit of dignity and privacy, a meager living. It was about oneness, and her understanding of who she surely was. It was a gift that surpassed class, prejudice, injustice, and inequality to tell the story of our true identity—when we have the courage to look beyond the elaborate facade we so often call reality.

A Brief Return to Eden

*The higher goal of spiritual living is not to amass a
wealth of information, but to face sacred moments*

RABBI ABRAHAM HESCHEL

Homecoming

It has become almost a cliché to talk about changing
things and making a difference, but the moment of
change is happening all the time, and we are inextricably
committed to it as part of the fabric of being alive. The truth is that
we are always making a difference: in the energy of our thoughts,
in how we do things as much as what we do, and even in the basic
act of listening, entering all relationships with an openness to
receive as well as give.

A few years ago I was walking in downtown Elkton with a
homeless woman who was living in the woods. As we conversed,
she drew us to a stop in front of a cafe. "How about we go inside,"
she invited, "I'll buy you a cup of coffee and we can talk there."

"She's living in the woods for crying out loud," I said to
myself, "I can't let her pay." So, I protested, politely to be sure, but
firmly, "I'll buy," was my response, "I insist." She turned on her
heel, as quickly as a dervish, facing me squarely with a look of
frustration and hurt; it's a vast understatement to say that she was
offended by my misguided spirit of charity. "Let me do it, please,
if you will" she chided, "I might be down on my luck but I was the
one who invited you; at least give me that respect."

Her rejoinder was not about coffee, money, pride, or
compassion: it was about being human, receptive—embracing the
dignity of the moment. She was not offering a polite sundry, but a
substantial gift, a rare chance to spin generosity my way in the

hope I would be gracious. Life's mission, our common vocation as people, is to know who we are, where we have come from, and where we are going. Our voyage may be through some troubled waters, but past the storms there is the wonder of glimpsing the paradise which is our native land. An intimation of another's true being in this life recalls our shared connection to the destiny of life itself, and to reckon that all change must come, not from adjusting others, but from within ourselves.

TRANSFORMATION:
Meeting Ourselves in Others

In Louisville, at the corner of Fourth and Walnut, in the center of the shopping district, I was suddenly overwhelmed with the realization that I loved all those people, that they were mine and I theirs, that we could not be alien to one another even though we were total strangers. It was like waking from a dream of separateness, of spurious self-isolation in a special world, the world of renunciation and supposed holiness. . . . This sense of liberation from an illusory difference was such a relief and such a joy to me that I almost laughed out loud. . .

THOMAS MERTON

ITALIAN IMMIGRANT NEIGHBORHOOD
PHILADELPHIA, 1925

A Man Who Would Listen

The Spirit in thee is a river.

THE HITOPADESA [Sanskrit book of stories]

Presence

His name was Ed, and his life's work centered on a sign. I met him in 1964 when I was a teenager working for the summer at St. Paul's House in New York City. He was a short man from Brooklyn; his hair was turning white with some pronounced black streaks left, full-bodied and combed back all the way with no part. He had a baggy look, at least his clothes gave that impression. He always wore suits—actually jacket and tie with noticeably mismatched pants—which I was pretty sure he got from a Chinese thrift shop he once recommended to me. He had a kind of Brooklyn underbite—his lower jaw jutted out a little further than his upper—and unlike most people who show their upper teeth when talking, Ed showed his lower. He smiled that way too: a humble kind of expression that put you at ease, and when he gave his enormous smile he showed all his teeth. I never knew where he lived, except that he lived alone and spartanly, and I still have no idea how he supported himself: but I do know what he did every day.

His mission was to walk. He walked slowly, steadily, and ceaselessly through the streets of New York, wearing a sandwich board sign almost as tall as he was. On the front in bold black letters: *Read your Bible. King James Version;* on the back side as he was walking away, you read*: For God so loved the world that he gave his only begotten son, that whosoever believeth in him should not perish, but have everlasting life. John 3:16.*

He didn't preach, but he stopped often as persons engaged him in conversation. The sign seemed loud, but, seemingly out of character, his voice and manner were gentle and quiet, and the open expression on his face was inviting, with a serenity which seemed almost otherworldly, in contrast to the bold display of words he wore. Rather than his preachments turning people away, passersby were actually attracted to him. He carried the sign, faithfully, persistently every day up and down the crowded, hot city sidewalks, and as he walked he exercised a unique gift of availability: easily drawn to a stop, often just to chat a little, and other times to listen as people poured out their broken hopes and dreams, sometimes in tears. Without interruption, preaching, or judgment, a fact most surprising for anyone who might have thought him a fanatic, he patiently heard it all.

I grew to admire him, even though I never knew what initially drew me to him—I suppose it was his open friendliness or maybe more than a little curiosity in wondering what motivated him in his inexorable task. I knew people who thought Ed was sick, condemned by a mental illness to his daily wandering, but whatever his reason, I walked many days with him on his pilgrimage, trying, as best as I knew how to see and understand with my feet.

As I walked, I was often puzzled by the hostility he sometimes got from people. Some ignored him, of course, out of self-consciousness or preoccupation with their own affairs, but others found him amusing, and I felt sorry for those who, seeing him only as a comical figure, missed the depth of his humanity. Still others were openly hostile, who yelled things like, "Get a job!" "Bigot!" "Go home, damn religious jerk!" And worse. I wondered what there was about Ed that set folks off, though it seemed to me those who showed the most hostility were also the most insecure, or perhaps the most resentful of someone devoid of the need to wear a mask of conformity. Whatever the reasons, Ed was unperturbed by these reactions; he seemed content to arouse at least some interest and response to his mission, and if he ever lashed out or answered back in anger at his detractors, I never saw it. In the depth of his civility in overlooking their ridicule, I began to see how much tolerance and courage his vocation required and that, behind the unkempt appearance, there was a character unique in its ability to meet and know all manner of people, and with them to share a heartfelt empathy.

When the summer was over, as I was getting ready to go back to school in Chicago, Ed honored me by making the trip across town to say goodbye. I had never seen him in any setting other than the street-walking. It was a quiet, warm summer evening in Manhattan, and we sat on the front stoop of the mission chatting about the summer past. As he stood up to take his leave, he surprised me with a gift: a beautiful old Stetson 10-gallon hat, boxed and in mint condition. It wasn't my style, actually I couldn't even imagine wearing it, and I did my best politely to refuse, but, in his gentle, persistent manner he would not be deterred, "You need a good hat," he insisted, "It gets cold in Chicago. Wear it!" How could I decline when he had gone to so much trouble to see me off? I took the hat with real appreciation, but I've always felt a little guilty about it, hoping he didn't give me something he indeed needed. To be honest, I never did wear it, but over time, seeing it on the closet shelf reminded me of him and what I learned from him on those walks. I kept it for many years before I gave it away to someone who needed it much more than I did, and even then I felt it was my way of passing on the generosity of a man who had changed my life by his example, sharing things like he shared himself, who he actually was, with strangers on sidewalks, hallowing the pavement with his openness.

I saw Ed one last time the following summer. Oddly enough, as destiny might have it, it was by complete chance that I ran into him on Market Street in my hometown of Philadelphia. He was Ed in true form. I saw him from a distance, walking slowly, intently, with his sandwich board sign, and seeing him, even from a long way off I thought, "It couldn't be him!" Then I quickly realized, "Who else?" I walked with him one last long summer afternoon; after that I never saw him again and I don't know what became of him. But I have become conscious since that he is not entirely gone. Part of him travels with me, and part of me still walks the street, from time to time, with him.

Over the years, I came to appreciate one last thing about Ed: his true message was never actually printed on that sandwich board. I don't know if anyone who ever saw him fixated much on what was written; they always focused on Ed himself, so that, like Marshall McLuhan's medium, the person became the message. Sometimes it doesn't matter so much what we do as who we are when we're doing it. His detractors may have been more intelligent, more politically correct, more sophisticated in their religious tastes, but Ed was by far more gracious, warmer, more apt to mourn earth's calamites, caring about the woes of persons who, surrounded by people in a crowded city, felt forgotten and alone. His ear was his weapon against a too-busy, self-important world, and it was always open to the chat of a distressed soul.

In the conviction of their intellectual superiority, or for whatever other reason, those who dismissed Ed as shallow were the same ones who never took the time to ask his name or smile at him. A few of us who genuinely got to know him understood the profound nature of his message: that he had found a path, a unique way of translating his esteem for people from inside to outside. He had discovered a method, a starting point for loving, and his calm walk was undoubtedly an earnest struggle to do just that. It was a mission to make a difference in the world by listening, and in hearing, to confirm others in their own worth; that those people were for the most part strangers, many scornful and hostile, only further confirmed the sincerity of his vocation.

I don't know what success Ed enjoyed if it can be measured by the quantity of people influenced. But if success is measured qualitatively by persistence, his achievement was magnificent, because he did try, every day, day after day, never losing a cheerful faith in himself or others. He may not have brought peace to the whole world, but he had the knack of bringing it to one person at a time. So, what gift he could not place directly into the hands of a God he couldn't see but yearned to love, he gave instead to strangers around him on the streets of Earth, as if it were indeed the mastermind of heaven itself who, by chance, had happened to walk by and catch his ear.

Richard's Diner

It is people who are important, not the masses.

DOROTHY DAY, *The Long Loneliness*

A church outside religion

It makes perfect sense for a member of a church, or other religious or interfaith community, to be outside religion. The model for this is Jesus himself, whose mission was to restore the promise of ourselves, and urge us to find within our own soul, and in others, the God which his religion had locked in a golden box.

In the words of William Blake, if ever anyone held eternity in the palm of his hand, it was Jesus. The simplest of living things became a sixth sense of wisdom to him: the flight of a sparrow, the potency in a seed, the complex beauty of a flower: everything opened a window on the generosity of the cosmos, the interrelatedness of all living things, and the bond of every part of life to the whole. Everyday experiences–the search for a lost coin, cleaning house, paying taxes, cooking a meal, engaging in commerce, even criminal activity—all served to transmit the nature of the life inside and around us: its splendor, universality, and resilience.

Paramount to Jesus, and most emphatically with those we think of as different, even alien, is our kinship with all other persons. His circle included social outcasts, foreign oppressors, domestic terrorists, the irreligious and nonreligious, and finally, as if these were not enough, he included all enemies. He corralled one and all into the household of God, and when questioned as to how we could possibly be expected to relate to one another he simply answered, *love*. The establishment of the faithful hauled him in, crowned him a blasphemer and killed him: if ever anyone was outside religion, it was Jesus.

Given this, it borders on the astonishing that Jesus found, within the religious institutions of his day, a forum and community of fellowship. His preference was to teach in the open air and at the crossroads of commerce. Yet he also took part in synagogue services, held court in the homes of religious leaders, and even in the famed Jerusalem temple itself: in these places, he found some of his most ardent followers, but alas also his most deadly critics. He was involved in the institutions of religion, he made use of its resources, but he was surely not a company man; although worshiped through the ages as Son of God, he was on the outs when it came to the special-interest group of dogma, and that is the most remarkable thing I know about him.

When I met Richard in 1984, he was a young man in his early twenties who was homeless and also mentally ill. To everyone he had been a normal, happy child and typical adolescent. In his late teens, however, his interior world began to disintegrate, and his life was overwhelmed with voices and fear. I first knew him when he was still struggling past the initial, turbulent years of schizophrenia. Once I found him sitting at a table, his face in his hands, totally despondent with a tangle of flypaper embedded in his bushy hair. He was tall, and somehow had gotten his hair stuck on one of the super-sticky strips hanging from the ceiling. As he became increasingly frustrated, struggling to get it out, it only got more enmeshed until, in utter defeat, he gave up, sat down, lit a cigarette, and, with flypaper raveled in his hair like a hapless babushka, he fell into the state of stoic despair in which I found him. With scissors, we worked together successfully to get it out, but that experience was typical of how even minor problems and setbacks could devour his existence.

One day, while he was still darkly preoccupied with his interior chaos, he was faced with an emergency. A friend was suddenly taken ill, and there was no one but Richard around to help. Although he had given up driving because of his own illness, and even as he was faced with a panic situation, he gently helped his stricken comrade into a car and drove several miles to the hospital, where he sat most of the day, quietly waiting and serving a needy neighbor with his presence. That evening I fully expected to find Richard broken down and disabled from the wrenching experience, but instead he appeared calmer and more peaceful than I had ever known him. Remarkably, the crisis, far from destroying him, had actually refreshed his beleaguered soul. How was it possible?

As I came to know him better, Richard revealed part of the answer himself. In the midst of a rambling conversation one day, he quietly interrupted the flow by suddenly looking directly into my eyes. "You know," he said, "I have thought about a church I would like to attend, if there were such a place." He then began to describe a kind of all-night diner in which a person, even without any money, could come and sit for a while, for as long as they wished. It wouldn't be terribly crowded as he imagined it was in the dead of night, yet it would be inhabited by friendly people who might bask in the quiet reassurance of each other's company. In this space, they might declare, with or without speaking, their mutual humanity.

The setting of the diner with its ordered tables and inviting murals, its reassuring smells of brewed coffee, fresh-baked pie, and breakfast any time, told of a place of refuge in warm-heartedness. Sharing hunger as a metaphor of our need for each other, Richard described, in longing phrases of desire, his ideal that a church should be without judgment or dress code, assumption of class or station, assuring unconditional acceptance of anyone. In this atmosphere of immanence, there would be no air of distance or flavor of the transcendent: his dreamy diner-church is encased from top to bottom in the familiar and comforting symbols of earth, people, and belonging. I thought of how Jesus might describe a house of worship indeed much like such a place, such a company of people, together; the liturgy would be the language of an honest heart, and the place might well be a step on the right side of heaven.

The Sacred History of our Everyday Life

The world is not comprehensible, but it is embraceable:
through the embracing of one of its beings.

<small>MARTIN BUBER</small>

One city

We sat in a circle in the chapel at Clairvaux Farm, folks from the Meeting Ground community and young people from a high school mission trip who had just finished a week of work camp. On a summer evening in 1998, after supper and just at sunset, we were sharing the meaning of the week's experiences. We usually had this meeting every Friday when there was a visiting group at the Farm, and there was no reason to think this one would be anything out of the ordinary. That is until Sam, a high school senior, slowly rose to his feet during a break in the conversation.

Sam was a serious-minded young man with a handsome, intelligent face and calm manner; he fit into the group well, was popular, and in every other way seemed to be an ordinary teenager from an affluent suburban church background. There was something in the way he spoke, an earnest emotional conviction that captivated us from the first sentence. He started talking slowly, almost reluctantly, as he recounted the story of how his consciousness had been turned inside-out between Sunday and Friday, the change coming as a result of a struggle: with himself, the meaning of service and above all in his relationship with an older man who had been homeless for years.

His foremost thought as the week began, was wondering what he was actually doing here at Meeting Ground, volunteering in place with homeless people. He didn't have any specific skills, especially for the landscaping job to which he had been assigned.

He was paired up to work with an older man named John, a resident of the community for many months: they were to start at the west fence and trim the thick growth which was engulfing it. The two had never met before and were worlds apart in their life experience and outlook. The young man was privileged, self-assured, and optimistic about his chances for a great future. John, a man in his fifties, down on his luck and depressed from a lifetime of dealing with prejudice, saw the world with apprehensive and fearful eyes; his future prospects appeared bleak to him, as his efforts and hard work so often seemed to amount to nothing. Homelessness became the end result: the product of a losing battle against his failures, his battered childhood, even his own skin. John was large in build, looking formidable but with a deferential nature; his personal problems were many, but he didn't talk openly about them, and if he smiled at you with his a full-faced grin you were instantly charmed.

They began their relationship that warm summer Monday morning with a problem neither could solve: they couldn't get the weed trimmer to work. Neither had used one before, and they grew increasingly frustrated, as the young man, assuming the older one at his age ought to know about such things, began to look down on him with a quiet contempt for his inadequacy.

"I was thinking to myself how stupid he was, and that was probably why he was homeless," Sam related in his story that Friday evening, "I figured he couldn't do anything right, and I was angry that I had been assigned to work with him. It made me wish I hadn't even come on the trip."

Eventually, with some outside help, they got it started and set to work. As they chopped overgrowth together in the increasing heat of the day, the young man woke up to something he hadn't expected. John was working diligently beside him, more than holding his own, and as the day progressed Sam had to struggle just to keep up with him. It was a surprise; he thought the *homeless man* would not have kept to the task, working awhile then giving up; he expected someone lazy. He later related how this puzzling realization unexpectedly jump-started his consciousness.

Late in the day, as they both wore down, they started to talk. John spoke about his own unsettled life and asked about Sam's hopes and dreams for the future; Sam surprised himself by his own eagerness to open up. He told things bottled up he never dared reveal to anyone before. He began to realize that the conversation was easy because the older man seemed genuinely to care about him and his life, as different as they were. They worked together the next four days, learning from and about each other, finally mastering what they had at first thought would be a mere weed-whacking assignment. By Friday, when the trimmer again wouldn't start, they looked at each other and laughed. They had come a long way from Monday: in a matter of days to an eternity of wisdom.

The chapel was almost dark as Sam spoke in the last light of a summer's day, but even so it was clear to see his eyes were welling with tears as his voice was choking with emotion. He began to cry outright when he told us how much he had misjudged John in the beginning, how he looked down on him and resented his having to work with such a seemingly incompetent person. He had wanted to be matched with someone he could look up to and actually learn from, and this disappointing start only stoked his resentment and disgust.

"How wrong I was," he continued, "John has taught me so much these last five days, and helped me to grow as a person; I will never be the same..." The room was crowded, but perfectly still; the story was riveting, and after he spoke there was a long, lingering silence and then a strong sense of realization. We were in the presence of something profound, a rare moment when the life-spirit moved among us so strongly that all felt connected, fully alive, aware of our singleness, together. John was also sitting in the circle; remaining quiet, head down, as we looked at each other with new eyes. How is it that two persons, so different in background, parentage, age, experience and destiny, could be so much alike, friends and kindred souls?

Maybe understanding the true measure of life is related to our capacity to see more of it. Perhaps churches, as all communities of faith, might be less fretful about dividing the hot-button issues and philosophies of society, and more absorbed in creating space for relationships and working to uncover the broad lands of the compassion we own. In that activity, the godhead, heretofore hidden—is uncovered at last. When we are captivated by our ironclad beliefs, we can repose in a kind of self-assured confidence. But love requires that we be wide open to the unexpected, confounding, even harsh new reality which before was inconceivable, yet now is altogether real and true. The persons, relationships, and circumstances which force us to lose our former certainties and prejudices are heaven-sent sages of what Dorothy Day once described as, "a revolution of the heart." Even as we are lost in the tangle of our own words mulling the insoluble mysteries, these prophets appear and give us new eyes.

To judge all that we see, hear and touch by the standard of a timeworn creed is only one city of understanding, and a lesser one at that. On the other side, there is a city of paradox and mystery, in which the impossible is granted, and dreams are breathed like air. The chronicle of that community is written in new beginnings as the book of the sacred history of our everyday life and the stories written in it by loves are never lost.

A Disquieting Neighbor

I hold a number of beliefs that have been repudiated by the liveliest intellects of our time. I believe that order is better than chaos, creation better than destruction. I prefer gentleness to violence, forgiveness to vendetta. On the whole I think that knowledge is preferable to ignorance, and I am sure that human sympathy is more valuable than ideology.

KENNETH CLARKE, *Civilization*

Sins of omission

The sheriff called on a cold January day in 2000, asking if we could provide any next-of-kin information for Jim. We learned then that he had been found dead that morning by the person who'd taken him in. Jim had been an on-and-off resident at Meeting Ground for the past two years, so we knew him well and were saddened to learn of his death, but not surprised. He had advanced congestive heart failure, was incredibly overweight, and chain-smoked. The news of his death reopened a painful issue. Two months earlier our community had struggled long and hard as to what to do about him. Eventually, in our utter weariness, we gave Jim a choice: change some of his ways or leave the community. Jim chose to leave.

Our decision was difficult, and came only after months of weighing options and trying to balance our responsibility to Jim with others in the community, including families with children. Some felt we should simply tell Jim to leave; others didn't think the situation warranted any intervention at all. The compromise made all of us feel we were acting *for his own good*. It seemed right at the time: now we wondered. Jim had visited the farm for the last time a few days before Christmas. He was sharing a small house with another formerly homeless person, and seemed content

94

with the simple refuge that this provided him. He liked coming back to visit at Meeting Ground; through his small bits of connection to the community he found a belonging which, having been disowned since childhood by his dysfunctional family, he needed so much.

Jim's entire life had been troubled, and had little to show for his sixty-plus years. No one seemed to know the exact reason for this. Jim himself probably never fully understood, but he carried a deep inner sadness, which may explain why he only paid lip service to reforming the harmful habits in his life. Perhaps junk food and cigarettes, his loyal, lifelong friends, were too dear to give up. Despite his brokenness, Jim was uncommonly kind and gentle. When he wished you *good morning* or *good night*, his entire face smiled as his eyes lifted with an openhearted gleam. From time to time, he would quietly, almost sheepishly, approach me, gently grab my arm, and ask me to pray for him; no one ever made a more sincere request, or expressed a deeper honesty of his need for other people. On those occasions when he reluctantly allowed himself to be hospitalized, and I would visit him there, I was always moved by how little he wanted to speak about his own trouble, and how eagerly he inquired about others by name.

He could indeed be endearing, but some in the community were insistent that Jim was getting away with too much: besides his overeating and smoking, they noted he was careless about his personal hygiene and keeping his sleeping area clean; what he needed, they asserted, was a stronger dose of what they called *tough love*. He had every right to feel angry with us for our determined crusade to reform him, but he never was. I can't recall him ever uttering a cranky word, let alone express any bitterness, except perhaps in the hospital when he itched to "get the hell out and go home." If he was ever insulted by our dogged attitude, he kept it to himself to the end.

I was one of those who felt Jim's contributions to the community far outweighed the discomfort he caused. I vividly remember the times I'd walk into the dining hall and see him straining to wash dishes or clean off a table. He had barely the strength to stand, but he took his chore assignments seriously, determined to do his best for others. Perhaps his greatest contribution was when anxious newcomers arrived in the community and found in his welcoming smile the assurance that everything would be okay for them. Jim allowed us to know him, and to know that our care meant something in his life. Finally, now with the news of his death, all the discussions, questions, and frustrations about making decisions for Jim *in his own best interest* were silenced. Jim had left us, slipping away quietly in his sleep, a final modest expression of his unassuming life. My last memory of him, from mere weeks before on his last visit to Meeting Ground, was a smile, a tight hug, and a roaring "Merry Christmas!"

The decisions were moot now, but the questions remained: did we, as a community, do right by him? Should we have asked him to leave sooner? Did we fail in our commitment to him by asking him to leave at all? When we later learned that Jim had been invited to live elsewhere, even while we were still debating what to do, did that lull us into an undeserved justification that we indeed had every right to insist he take advantage of this opportunity to move on?

These questions around Jim also opened the way to larger issues. Where is the line between wanting to help someone change for the better and respecting that person's autonomy and individuality, even if it takes self-destructive forms? What's the difference between deciding you don't have the right to intervene in another person's life, and then to watch them stumble without reaching out to catch them or act to help cushion their fall? To these and the other questions, there are no ready or easy answers, but one thing is crystal-clear to me: though Jim's personality was irksome, sometimes demanding, it also manifested gentleness, quiet good humor, longing loneliness, and quick capacity to forgive. Simple acknowledging of those qualities in Jim may be the closest I ever came to answering the question we were in actual fact asking: what is the meaning of such disquieting persons in our lives?

Sometimes, just to stretch my own soul, I might fantasize that Jesus would appear at Meeting Ground in the guise of a social worker or fire inspector, clipboard in hand, checking off the quality and sincerity of our care for others; clearly the daydream of an afternoon with little else on the schedule. Giving this thought another twist, I might imagine that he would instead show up as a troubled person, his or her odd ways inviting snickers of contempt or heads shaken in pity, thinking how lucky we are not to be in their shoes.

I suppose the whole idea of Jesus returning and rubbing shoulders with us like that is a little far-fetched, but I can't help but remember how so many of Jim's personal qualities were like those of brother Jesus. Jim did not just pretend to be gentle or forgiving—it was genuine; his tolerance for the faults of others, the product of so much hardship in his own life, and his love for other people was rare in its utter sincerity. All that aside, Jim was a creature of some revolting habits, and for that I am certain he was not a revisiting Jesus.

Well, then again, maybe I'm not that sure. If the Nazarene were to be with us as a difficult and perplexing person, it would certainly test the true nature of our vaunted kindness and compassion. Would I welcome such a visitor whose mere presence challenges a tenuous self-certainty? Ultimately it could be a matter of the distance we place between ourselves and others. Does violating an arbitrary standard of human conduct mean that a person is no longer an image of the divine? I ask these questions knowing full well that Jim would never have raised the same doubts about me if the tables had been turned; he seemed always to have room in his life for us all, even as we persisted in our conditional acceptance of him.

So maybe my imagination is not as wildly off-course as I like to pretend. For I am certain that knowledge of the deepest meaning of human love, which comprehension is the holy grail of life itself, is indeed as close as that disquieting neighbor who demands, with neither justification nor apology, our kind and generous affection.

A Majestic Interruption

Human beings are so made that the ones who do the crushing feel nothing; it is the person crushed who feels what is happening. Unless one has placed oneself on the side of the oppressed, to feel with them, one cannot understand.

SIMONE WEIL

Integrity once lost

The possibility of virtue begins with discontent.

There is something so intimidating about a room full of adults sitting on a committee, about to hold a meeting. Once such a consultation has begun, even late arriving members are timid, tiptoeing contritely, sheepishly smiling with a half-raised hand gesture of greeting and a read-my-lips apology for being late. Such is the awe of a group, seated. Persons who sit on such boards, or any association which identifies itself with a power, are engaging in the subordination of individual decision-making to the process of a group. At its best, it can be a powerful means of working together, to share a common mind in doing a job. At its worst, it can become a certain type of moral protective coloration, excusing individual members from personal responsibility, thinking and deciding without the messy restraints ordered by tender empathy. Organized human endeavor may not be possible without committees, but it remains the responsibility of those who sit on them to put their own integrity first. Group consensus can be achieved either by mutual subordination of truth, or by together coming home to ourselves.

One evening I was part of a committee that was just sitting down for such a meeting. In the solemnity of our convening, in the midst of the big business of parsing minutes and raising the minutia of an agenda to high importance, the door opened and God entered the room in the form of a nine-year-old girl. She stood in the doorway scowling, hands-on-hips, visibly angry. "I want to know," she demanded, "why me and my mom have to leave the shelter tomorrow." She repeated the challenge several times in different ways, her eyes searching around the table for the bravery of a reply.

There was none. How could anyone answer what was not merely a question, but a cry of anguish from a young girl whose surface indignation only briskly hid her intense hurt and fear. The decision to ask her mother to leave, we thought, had been easy and needed; some asserted she had simply broken the rules; she was uncooperative and a negative influence on others. It was a straightforward matter of facts, and presumably fairness, a decision which had to be made.

Straightforward, that is, until the unexpected entrance—a powerful majestic interruption, a riveting disturbance in a well ordered universe. In her sovereignty, God brought us home to ourselves and challenged us to deliberate further, this time in the presence of a single person who spoke from the raw essence of who she was, without well-bred fabrication. Perhaps we had made the right decision, perhaps not. She made us uneasy in our smug comfort: troubled about a judgment we had made so casually removed from the terror of her homelessness, and her courage only magnified the shabbiness of our prior deliberation. What is a system; what is a committee, after all? It's only a bowl for the food of human relationships. How it functions is critical; it can nourish or it can deprive and starve the same ones to whom it is beholden.

The mother of all majestic interruptions has to be when Jesus entered the outer court of the vast Jerusalem temple at Passover, the holiest of religious observances, when tradition and the weight of sacred authority overshadowed all—attacking the money changers, interrupting in an angry denunciation the status quo of the all-wise *Sanhedrin*, perhaps the mother of all committees. When he did this he signed his own death warrant; he knew it, he predicted it would happen. He had interrupted an establishment so exclusive in its deliberations, so convicted of its own infallibility, and so removed from outside opinion that it considered itself the mouth of God. Jesus, standing at the door, hands on hips, couldn't move them.

It is better for a system to perish than that it wrongfully, and without apology, maim one human person. Why? Because a person carries the possibility and promise of all that is holy, and to allow one purposefully hurt, is to harm all people everywhere. But, we stand assured, if it had been our committee back then, when Jesus intruded so blatantly on our business, we surely would have taken heed.

Life's Highest Adventure

*Anything can happen, anything is possible and likely.
Time and space do not exist. On a flimsy ground of
reality imagination spins out and weaves new patterns.*

AUGUST STRINDBERG, *The Dream Play*

A necessary frankness

Embodied in the practice of virtue is the spirit of adventure. Virtue needs adventure because it requires the material of new and creative relationships, expansion of old boundaries, and a broader view of God. This passion for exploration is life's underlying energy, calling us away from the reinforcement of a stale status quo to a spirituality of life which engages the stranger in ourselves and kinship with others. The great spiritual masters were immersed in adventure, their lives are replete with the stories: Buddha's abandonment of the palace for a life of poverty, Jesus' stoning at Nazareth, Abraham's displacement from Ur, Muhammad's flight from Mecca, Paul's Mediterranean journeys, Esther's regal heroism, and the celebrated love of Ruth and Boaz, just to name a few—the list could go on forever. The rush of the unexpected is the nourishment of living. It is the turbulent factor, the challenging force that will not allow our growth to cease. It is the impetus that moves us on to that which is our soul's original desire: the excitement of coming home, the chance of fully realizing love, and the only road I know to heaven.

Nick was a 17-year-old high school senior who came to Clairvaux Farm for a week around 1994 with his church's summer mission trip. He was not eager; in fact, he arrived complaining about how he felt put out to be doing work for others which, as he kept repeating, "they should very well be doing for themselves." He was born into a family of comfortable means, and he hadn't seen much of life on the other side of the tracks. He joined the mission team, not motivated by virtue, but to be with his girlfriend. That's how the week began, but by week's end everyone saw a profound change in him. No longer arrogant and complaining, he quietly became the best worker of the group, sometimes performing his tasks with tears in his eyes, and the story behind his transformation was remarkable in its speed. I won't easily forget the sultry hot evening, temperature near 100, sitting on benches under a pair of tall oak trees, as an emotional Nick told us what had happened to him only a day before.

With no interest in getting to know anyone in the community, he griped his first two days about having to help *unworthies.* Wednesday was different. On that day everything changed. It was a steaming-hot Eastern Shore summer afternoon. He was walking across the front lawn, a grassy area as big as a soccer field. As chance would have it, also walking across in the opposite direction was a five-year-old girl who was living at the Farm with her family. Brandy had never known a real home, or a period when her living was not filled with abuse, chaos, and sadness. Nick's story was polar opposite. His background was stable, and his future assured. These two vastly different people, one tall, the other short, just happened to cross paths on the sunny green that lazy afternoon.

They stood face to face in front of each other, she smiling as broadly as he looked puzzled. For no other reason than the habit of a girl needing love, she held her arms out wide and asked Nick for a hug. Awkwardly hesitant at first, he reached down slightly. She jumped into his arms, and he held her a short time. But in a moment of stunning empathy, the kind that changes a person's life forever in an instant, when Nick relaxed his arms, Brandy would not let go. In that split second of time, as Nick told the story to his friends the following night, sheer emotion overwhelmed him. It wasn't the hug itself, it was the not letting go—that the little girl clutching his chest would not release her arms, holding tightly for dear life, as if in that one embrace she had seized, for a one and only time, the whole universe. From then on, for the rest of the week and into his untold future, Nick told us he knew he would be haunted by what had happened. He would, for the rest of his years, continue to explore depths within himself for a love, an unyielding love, steadfast to not let go. Two people, seemingly worlds apart, discovered they were extraordinarily alike in reaching for something in another person they yearned to find within themselves. They perhaps both knew, each in the other, that in the moment it was themselves they embraced, hoping to hold on forever. Conversion comes to mind; the mainstay of the old-time religion: that in one single instant of time, all things might become new.

Brandy went on to confound the limited expectation of her circumstances. She did well in school in spite of ongoing homelessness. A dozen years later I was in my office when the phone rang and the caller ID indicated that it was the *Cecil Whig*, the local newspaper. To my surprise it was Brandy; she was doing an internship with the paper as a photographer and she called to ask if she could do a photo story on Clairvaux Farm. My mind went back in time: "The place where she hugged Nick so tightly that day," I thought, "How far she has come, how very far indeed." So many children who have experienced such homeless chaos never even make it to high school, let alone graduate—but I was there when, to boisterous applause, she crossed the stage and received her diploma.

Her story is far from finished. Brandy still struggles to balance sporadic attendance at college with working and keeping a roof over her head. And she contends every day with the grief from her years of homelessness as a child. She is still seeking to fully answer the question her own heart raised with Nick that summer afternoon: where is the love that is never lost? Once in speaking to his pupils, Socrates asked what it meant to *know thyself*, a phrase inscribed on the portico of the temple of Apollo at Delphi: *"And what do you suppose a person must know to know himself, his own name merely? Or must he consider what sort of creature he is?"* Perhaps the path to knowing who we are begins with the transforming realization that we are loved: the embrace that will not let us go. It may well be true that we will all find, one day or another, this is the exact sort of creature we are.

The practice of virtue is an adventure because with each new day there is the possibility of finding that pearl of great price: the expansion of love's perimeters. In the possibility of each new discovery, and in the exchange of it, we are sublimely moved, exposed to a bit of heaven real enough to hold. And in the truest part of who we are, we sense that this is our life's work, the only task that matters, which in its practice, truly satisfies. Virtue requires us to be open to the possibility of simply making room in our life every day for the one who appears to be, on the surface, from ourselves, so different.

Masquerade

How lovely to think that no one need wait a moment, we can start now, start slowly changing the world! How lovely that everyone, great and small, can make their contribution toward introducing justice straightaway... And you can always, always give something, even if it is only kindness!

ANNE FRANK, *Diary of a Young Girl*

Unleashed pretense

I have known Lucille on and off for over a quarter century. But I did not know her when she was younger and dreaming of life as never-ending spring. She is my age, among the first of the baby boomers, so it's easy for me to visualize Lucille say, in the sixth grade or as a high school sophomore, or laying on the beach getting a tan while listening to Elvis in the early 60s hangover from the un-fabulous 50s.

As I said, I did not know her then. I only met her when she was middle-aged, homeless, and angry most of the time. It was the toxic brew of a bewildering childhood, a failed marriage and resulting depression all blended, like in some dark madcap comedy, into a breakdown of mind and spirit. When I first met Lucille around 1987 it was just after dawn at Wayfarers' House. I was annoyed to hear the obnoxious noise of an un-muffled power mower breaking the early morning peace. When I looked out a back window I saw Lucille clad in a long pink bathrobe and furry slippers pushing hard at the mower, flattening the heavy wet grass. She did things like that—as the time when the police found her standing in the middle of a highway. She was only trying to get across the street, she casually explained, but stopped at the double yellow line trying to decide whether stepping over it would be legal.

Lucille was different. She never smiled. If you tried to strike up a conversation she would tilt her head to one side as she lifted it slightly, looking out the corner of one eye while raising the other as if to ask, "What's your real angle?" With it all, she still had the fine symmetry and stature of an attractive and poised woman. Wrinkles, gray hair, and a drawn look from years of chain-smoking could not fully hide the remains of a winsome and energetic strength she once had in abundance. On the rare occasions when she would discuss her life, she spoke in veiled generalities, vaguely referring to financial reverses and romantic betrayals of a young woman from an affluent home whose parents who were cold, distant, and demanding. She married young: it was apparently short and not so sweet. The past pressed in on a woman now cynical and jaded, trusting no one but especially suspicious of anyone wanting to help. She was proud, stubborn, and guarded.

It was especially difficult to strike up a casual conversation with her. She was bristling with defenses. We all wear masks, but hers was like an elaborate fancy dress costume ball. She sneered a lot, usually cued by the things that made other people smile. Rather than talk about her pain she vented her deep frustration in angry outbursts which typically started with a sudden shout, followed by a long vacant stare, then an escalating crescendo of venom directed at everyone and anyone: from the President of the United States to the unlucky person who had dared engage her in conversation. There was no end to it. Once the outburst began the only hope was to vacate the area, leaving Lucille fuming alone at the table, cigarette in hand, two fingered (sometimes one fingered) fist waving in the air until, like a spent volcano, it all settled into a self-exhausted smolder.

It was sometime in the summer of 2005, and Lucille was again homeless and living with us at Clairvaux Farm. We were in the middle of mission trip season and we had a group from Allentown, Pennsylvania staying with us. It was a typical group of dedicated church young people: except for Susan. Susan was different. She was a 16-year-old girl who had tagged along as a guest of someone in the group. She was troubled and distracted and, much like Lucille, she wore her anger on her sleeve along with a constant tension on her face. She too had the same manner of sitting at the porch table like a bored houseguest, nursing a cigarette in a menacing solitude that passersby were afraid to disturb. Even her friend found it difficult to have a conversation with her and by midweek we began thinking of sending her home early on the bus. Many at the farm were having the same thought: *Lucille junior*.

So it happened on Wednesday evening after dinner that someone from the Farm community came running over to the Chapel where I was busy rearranging chairs. Half out of breath and leaning on the door he said, "You'd better come over to the dining Hall right away, there may be trouble."
"What's up?"
"It's Lucille… and Susan… you know, the girl…"
"What about them?"
"Whoever who made the chore schedule wasn't thinking; they put those two together to wash dishes tonight… someone set Lucille off and the last we saw her she was headed into the kitchen loaded for bear. God in heaven help us when those two get together!"

I stopped with the chairs right away and we both dashed over to the dining hall. In my mind I could only see a red-faced, fuming Lucille encountering a slowly simmering Susan standing next to a grotesque pile of dirty dishes—a perfect set up for World War III. When I walked into the kitchen I was stopped in my tracks all right, but not how I had expected. Lucille and Susan were standing at the sink. Indeed there were stacks of plates running over in the suds, but they were both smiling with broad and excited delight, washing and drying away. They were chatting like long lost friends about this and that, including the most personal things—their lives, hopes, even their disappointments—and laughing. It was one of those jaw-dropping moments, like remembering where you were when you first heard about the moon landing, forever etched in memory. They were best buddies for the rest of the week: aging Lucille and young Susan, leaving all of us who knew them scratching our heads in the wonder of it all.

What had they accomplished by themselves that the best professionals—psychiatrists, social workers, clergy—could only fantasize achieving? For Lucille and Susan, the masquerade ended with meeting; and the meeting happened because they, each one, on first looking into the face of the other, smiled and dropped the deeply embedded act as if shedding a useless heavy coat on a warm day. Nobody wants to be an object of charity, as much as charities need such persons. We would all rather be the helpers, not the needy one. Lucille and Susan had invented a context in which each of them could be helped in meeting the other. Most times, I think, we are reluctant to admit the hunger of our own souls. To express our own neediness and emptiness makes us vulnerable and far too open to disappointment and pain. The act of giving makes us feel better, but the act of *meeting* gives us the freedom to remove the mask and be human again. Meeting each other liberates us, and in this new freedom is our hope for change. Such a powerful gift can only be given when we see ourselves in the glint of another's eye.

A meal is significant not only because we have to eat in order to live, but because it is a context of opportunity. Cast among the sounds of pots and dishes is laughter, gentle kidding, and sometimes a life-changing bit of conversation. And who may know what dreams may come, perhaps, in the smile of a stranger by a kitchen sink? Maybe that's why we know more of Jesus' teaching at meals than in churches. At the table all things are possible, even rich and poor may meet together. And that's what Jesus once said heaven was like: a table which must be full.

We had tried so hard and for so long to make Lucille what most would consider normal, but she preferred her mask of indignation to the polished and self-assured delusions of professionals who try to help without the risk of meeting: she wanted to be embraced, not fixed. She knew she was a sanctity of one—an individual unlike any other who had ever lived or would live. The price of her liberation was to give up the masquerade: a gamble only Susan's welcome made possible. Lucille and Susan met themselves in each other and were transformed.

IMAGINATION: A New Heaven...

The clothes we had usually didn't fit well because children grow fast and the little bits of money that we had were not used for us to have comfortable things. We lost so many things; pictures, keepsakes, pets; can you imagine it? We rarely got to have meals around a table, rarely had beds to sleep on and rarely had space of our own. We couldn't get to gatherings or children's parties to be included and have fun. You see, when you have to ask people to take you places for necessities then you shouldn't ask them to take you places for fun; that is too much usage of a resource that is not your own.... The time I spent with my family at the homeless shelters was over a period of 4 years, from when I was ages 10 to 14. I hated being at the homeless shelters as much as I hated living in other people's homes.

TRACEY McCAW

Then I saw a new heaven and a new earth, for the first heaven and the first earth had passed away...

REVELATION 21:1

THE BOLDLY LIVING TREE

A Small Girl's Stand for Justice

Mankind's history has proved from one era to another that the true criterion of leadership is spiritual. People are attracted by spirit. By power, persons are forced. Love is engendered by spirit. By power, anxieties are created.

MALCOLM X

A little determination

The civil war in El Salvador was raging in the spring of 1987, when I was part of an interfaith delegation which accompanied Salvadoran refugees from the Mesa Grande camp in Honduras on a return to their war-devastated villages in Chalatenango province. Many who were going home were survivors of the brutal massacres at the *Sumpala* and *Lempe* rivers in which, attempting to flee from their own nation's army, they were caught in the cross fire of battle and brutally gunned down by soldiers of two countries as they tried to escape. Those who lived then began a decade of bleak homelessness as refugees; they had seen the full ugly face of political, economic, and social injustice and I wanted to know more of how they survived and endured it.

They had been struggling to return home for ten arduous and exasperating years, facing the hostility of the Salvadoran government, their own fear of torture, reprisal and death, and the timid bureaucratic process of UNHCR (United Nations High Commissioner for Refugees), under whose protection they had been living. In the course of their Honduran exile, they had cultivated, like their matchless skill in growing *maize*, courage and persistence in the face of constant danger with an unshakable faith in themselves capable of moving mountains. In their extraordinary *comunidades religiosas de base,* base communities of faith, they had grown together into a neighborhood of uncommon confidence in who they were and what they were capable of achieving. As remarkable as I found this, coming from a culture that promulgates charity in place of liberation—it was a young girl, maimed in the war, who most dazzled my imagination.

I first noticed her soon after we had entered the camp, as the refugees were busy packing and disassembling buildings in preparation for their return. She looked to be about nine or ten years old, although in asking around no one was actually quite sure of her age. Many of the children in the camp were *adopted* into families after having been orphaned in the war. She never spoke, the terrors of war had rendered her mute, and her body was severely deformed from shrapnel; she walked with considerable effort using a thick carved stick as a crutch. In spite of her frailty, she was an integral part of the community, coming and going like the other children, doing chores, fully accepting her role and being in turn accepted by everyone.

On the date which had been set for their return to El Salvador, no trucks or busses arrived, as had been promised by UNHCR, and the refugees were becoming anxious. Sensing that they had been betrayed once again by the patronizers who always decided what was best for them, they knew they were at a crossroad—if they did not seize the moment, exercising initiative on their own responsibility, they might never get home. They decided on a bold step. Three hundred members of the community organized, ignoring the promised buses, to march out of the camp some 10 miles to the town of San Marcos to the local headquarters of the UNHCR. There they intended to occupy the office and press their demand to return home.

And march they did. They walked in the hot sun and the pouring rain; they walked out of the camp knowing the Honduran military could, on a whim, decide to shoot. They marched past sand bags, bunkers, and machine guns aimed at them at the main gate; they marched past heavily armed soldiers in full battle gear who lined the road from the camp; in double columns almost a quarter mile long they marched behind the flag of El Salvador.

They marched into a hostile town and met with officials who proved to be as intransigent as ever, unmoved neither by their courage nor the harshness of their ordeal. All three hundred were forced by the army from the UN offices into a one hundred square foot open pavilion under tight military guard. There they were compelled to live for weeks, to sleep through cold nights on a bare concrete floor, and except for their fellow refugees at the camp who brought them food every day they might have starved, as no one seemed prepared to give them anything.

It was on the first day of this imprisonment, after having walked with the refugees on their extraordinary journey, that I turned a glance and saw something that made a chill run down my spine. Astonishingly, across that bleak pavilion, I spotted the young girl on the crutch. With my mind in a whirl, it began to sink in that she also had made the long and perilous walk from the camp, through the heat and rain and past the guns; perhaps she had walked partway, then was carried by others, I wasn't sure, but here she was—one of three hundred, marching for the justice of going home.

She stirred all our deepest emotions. As she struggled to walk, herself so challenged and exposed, shifting here and there around that tiny prison she questioned the mighty. Why this military guard to keep her in check? How could she, who could barely walk, who only wanted to go home, create such an atmosphere of threat to established order? "Why," I asked myself, "is she the cause of paralyzing consternation at the highest levels of government?"

She was like Jesus. Standing alone before unjust judges, he countered the prestige of wealth and power with the simplicity of silence, relying on his presence alone, and the spirit within. Nothing is truer, nor more potent than our self-awareness—the unfolding of a majesty which can't be suppressed, and against which all pretenders to greatness count for nothing.

It took some time, but the authorities grudgingly relented, and the dispossessed of Mesa Grande finally returned home: the sheer weight of their conviction had tipped the scales in their favor.

In the determined exercise of their faith in themselves, the powers of the earth stood back and made way. The small girl who had silently and courageously stood her ground was with them. Her road to justice and theirs, began when, abandoned by all others, they seized the moment that their redemption would be just-us.

The Church and the Cotton Lamb

I am neither spurred on by excessive optimism nor in love with high ideals, but am merely concerned with the fate of the individual human being that infinitesimal unit, on whom, if we read the meaning of the Christian message aright, even God seeks this goal.

CARL JUNG

Hand-made conviction

Sometimes in the evening, when the wind begins softly to come up, and night settles in, a person can see more clearly than in bright daylight. We perceive by touch, the chill on our skin, and by the smell of the night air. And in the quietness of the time, we are sometimes afraid; afraid for ourselves, afraid for our children, afraid for Mother Earth, and for the sacred memory of the love which ties all together as one. And we are sometimes fearful for our own religion. In our utter need we may find ourselves thinking: if religion can't save us what on earth or in heaven can?

My friend Terry who grew up in Appalachia once told me that when she was a girl in Sunday School she was brought unexpectedly close to heaven through the experience of making a lamb out of colored paper, paste and cotton. She was in the church, surrounded by its aura of ancient wisdom and tradition. But its vast, cold emptiness and its far-away God were not what she drew on for her virtue. She was the source. She was creating something out of her being, from within herself, something new and complete: a work of her hands and heart which spoke of her own immense power of expression. Some things we must do on our own, and our happiness is not in relishing someone else's brilliance, but the satisfaction of forging a new beginning.

Likewise, in our own hands, uncertain as they may seem, lies the same power of soul and revelation... and the possibility of moving beyond the cold air of our hushed religion which surrounds us on every side.

The Feeding Bowl Community

*For the bees he set honey and wine in the winter, lest
they should feel the nip of the cold too keenly; and bread
for the birds, that they all, but especially "my brother
lark," should have joy of Christmastide.*

ON ST. FRANCIS OF ASSISI, *The Little Bedesman of Christ*

Doing hope

In late January, around 2002, a surprise snowstorm caught
us with fifteen inches of cover, followed by ice. At
Clairvaux Farm, where we were used to spreading out over twenty
acres, our lives were suddenly reduced to heated rooms, shoveled
pathways, and happily, a steep back hill for sledding. Even in the
inhospitable season, the front porch of the dining hall, although
unheated, remained a gathering place, especially before and after
meals, and not just for us humans.

As the snow covered every inch of bare ground, the birds
began searching for food, as did our ongoing congress of stray
cats. The story began around a feeding bowl, which was a fixture
at Clairvaux Farm in those days, set out on the porch for Jake, our
resident beagle; he owned the corner with the bowl and blankets,
and while the food was rightly his, when he wasn't there everyone
else felt quite free to help themselves. The arrival of snow raised
this tradition to the level of high drama. With Jake otherwise
occupied, a number of small birds, wrens and juncos at first, began
rapidly hopping in through the door and across the porch to the
feeding bowl, pecking up their fill and dashing out as quickly as
they had come in. The porch was screened so they couldn't fly in;
they had to enter through a floor-level hole across from the bowl.
One after another they marched as orderly as penitents lined up for
confession, in and out of the porch, back and forth to the feeding
bowl, only interrupted when Jake or the cats reappeared; then a

give-and-take came into play, an elegant timing, so that everyone—birds, cats, and Jake—knowing their place in the order, took a little bit, then moved on to make room for others. The whole business was as uncanny as the farm itself.

Because it is set in the country on Maryland's Eastern Shore, Clairvaux Farm is a unique kind of place for a homeless community: it's a beautiful setting, but the deep snow was always a distinct hardship, especially so in the early years. It sometimes took days to get the lane and paths cleared, and we could never remove all the ice, making even short walks treacherous for people who had difficulty getting around, and downright impossible for wheelchairs. Sharing this adversity gave everyone a particular empathy for the birds in their distress. Everyone also knew that when the snow melted, things would get back to normal, and the birds would abandon their perilous porch-hopping. They only did it because they were fighting to stay alive.

Hard times, though it may be our sheer survival which is at stake, can open fresh vistas of reality: even the possibility of new, sometimes highly unlikely, relationships—including the one with ourselves. Watching a small bird engaging in the creative art of survival was the stuff of a parable: a story Jesus might have told. When life proves especially difficult, they increase their capacity for taking risks, moving into new and unfamiliar environments, boldly facing hazards, even challenging what they would ordinarily flee. Their exaggerated darting at the feeding bowl showed they must have been afraid, yet in spite of this they were bold, daring things one could never imagine them doing before the snow.

A sense of loss, sometimes extreme, comes with privation, along with fear of being alone; we become alienated from what before was a predictable and safe world. Our once familiar landscape is gone, and we may begin to fear for our actual survival. That dread, like a stalking predator, suddenly becomes an unwelcome attendant as are enveloped by the blizzard, feeling surrounded and about to be overwhelmed. We can overcome only when we see that we are at the threshold of another kind of opportunity. We are alone, yes, but not truly, never completely. A door always opens, and it is the one that leads to our own center, our core, boundless and unchanging. As we walk through to meet the challenge, we find a new way to go deeper into the place where we know that all is well. Though it may look bleak and cold all around, always within us is the consolation that we have a place at that same table—feeding bowl if you will—set for us before the earth was in flower, and to know that we don't have far to go before the mean season ends, and we find ourselves back at home, larger than we ever imagined.

Dave and the Denim Dress

*I had reasoned this out in my mind, there was one of two
things I had a right to, liberty or death; if I could not
have one, I would have the other.*

HARRIET TUBMAN

Creating change

O ver the years, I have known many persons who have
accepted homelessness as the best alternative for their
lives. It's not that they like being rained on, or shivering under the
stars in a sleeping bag, but it's a choice among few others: being
destitute not to be subject to another's rules—to remain
independent. Being homeless is to face limited options, but choice
is always our regal birthright, and sometimes the alternative is to
be a *knight of the road.* These restless souls are not so much
homeless by choice, as through an association which is demanded
by who they are. They are by nature quiet, somewhat reclusive, dirt
poor and fiercely self-determining. Although they may avail
themselves of the hospitality of a warm shelter in winter, the first
sign of spring will find them back on the road or in the woods,
returning to a colony of one.

Dave was one such man who was living at Clairvaux Farm
during the winter of 2003. Even before the first hint of spring he
was preparing again for his lone journey. He left without a word
although we knew he was getting ready; he slipped away quietly
one early morning, as the forsythia was blooming, walking out the
long front lane, down the road and back to himself. Over his
shoulder he carried his few belongings in a homespun denim
satchel with buttons instead of a zipper.

The day he left, someone recalled that just a few weeks
before Dave had noticed, and quickly appropriated, a long blue

jean skirt in a pile of donated clothing. Folks smiled at the time, wondering what he could possibly want with a woman's discarded clothing. He dropped out of sight for a day or so while he assiduously cut and sewed it to his liking, and when he was done the skirt had become a duffel bag. When I heard what had happened, I thought that even if a shiny, brand-new valise had been available, Dave probably still would have preferred to make his own satchel out of the castaway dress. Anyone could see that a regular canvas bag would have been so much stronger, more rainproof, convenient and serviceable, but it would also have lacked the imprimatur of Dave's own hand. The bag he made was entirely his: not just his possession, it was his offspring. From an item no one wanted, he fashioned a thing of value.

This story speaks for itself in its straightforwardness, but there is something inspiring about Dave that I have a hard time putting my finger on: perhaps it's the romance of a life that has learned to make the entire world home, or appreciation of his freedom, or because he has found so much comfort in the vast territory of his own soul. Whatever the reason, finally, who could not help but admire, almost to the point of envy, the person who makes a radical shift of life, requiring only an old denim dress to do so?

The Birdhouse Incident

If you have come to help me, you are wasting your time,
but if you have come because your liberation is bound
up with mine, then let us walk together.

LILLA WATSON

Requisite imagination

We know there is immense power in imagination, but, realists that we are, we sometimes belittle this mainstay of life. We dismiss it by saying things like, "It was just in our imagination," when we want to assert that something has no tangible truth or importance. Yet, do we experience any reality at all apart from our creative posturing of it? Is not our inventive perception of the world, drawn from a myriad of possibilities, that which creates what is real? May we not as easily think the world around us to be hostile and threatening as to dream that it is filled with splendor and opportunity? Children are confident in creativity, envisioning a world shaped to their dreams and desires. So where in life do we so lose our way to rely, no longer on the vast power of our own creativity, but on what passes for a mass assent of reality?

Homeless persons, especially, often are not permitted the luxury of imagining, certainly not to dream. They are frequently made to feel that they have become homeless because they haven't faced reality hard enough, and that now is the time, as they say, to get a grip with the real issues of life: jobs, houses, habits, and the like. Yet, how much of this is possible to achieve or obtain without the driving, penetrating zeal of our interior vision? Imagination turns the four walls of a house from a shell to a home, and our heart invents the unique things that make it so. If there is no dream, there is only drudgery.

So it happened one early spring day in 2001 that a group of kids at Clairvaux Farm got it in their mind to make a birdhouse, and they begged Elmer, a fair carpenter, to help them. Elmer was a classic curmudgeon, gruff and solitary one day, friendly as a cat in a fish camp the next; one never knew. He was on his best behavior around children, though, like many parents estranged from their own kids and missing too much of their growing up. He always kept a bittersweet place open in his life for all youngsters, and they sensed it. He said no to making the birdhouse, much as he might have wanted to, because he was so pressed with the complex demands of getting his life back together. He had gotten a job, but as transportation to work was an ongoing problem, he was close to losing it. One thing led to another in his efforts to keep his momentum going, and before long he wound up incarcerated: arrested for driving an unregistered vehicle, which triggered the system to nab him on a slew of unpaid violations. In the blink of an eye, he lost career, car, and savings, along with his delicately crafted plan to get back on his feet. Released from jail, he was back at the Farm and back to square one. Time to face reality, one might say, but where to start when the imagination is no more alive than a meatloaf on steroids? At this low point in his life, Elmer looked to the dream he had put on the shelf: he needed the birdhouse more than anything else.

It is a breathtaking function of the human soul, which believes in, and yearns for sunrise, even in the middle of an endless night. Even so, you might imagine my feeling when, walking by the back woods, glancing at an overgrown wild cherry tree, my eye was caught by the unexpected sight of a massive, blue, two-story birdhouse. The details of it were striking. It wasn't just thrown together; it was obviously made from various pieces of wood, drawn from here and there, some would call it scrap, but it was so neatly built with a keen eye for detail and an artful flair. It was mounted solidly in the tree by someone who cared that its inhabitants would be secure and on solid footing. It was even slightly tilted at an angle to let rainwater drain away. Everyone who saw it looked twice and again; it was that striking. It drew admiration like a magnet.

After all, though, one could say it was just a commonplace thing: birdhouses are everywhere, mostly manufactured to be cheaply gotten in the Wal-Marts of this world. But this was no ordinary birdhouse, not even like the custom-made ones. It was like Thoreau's artist in the city of Kouroo who was disposed to strive after perfection in fashioning a flawless walking stick, a work of both inspired hands and longing soul. Of course, it was not exclusively Elmer's work. It also belonged to the kids who asked him to do it; they were its soul and inspiration. In their eagerness to build a house for passing birds, even as they and their families were struggling to find their own homes, they unwittingly expressed a universal theme of the human heart: all life is one in its yearning to imagine, dreaming of its place of eternal belonging.

Every sentient being has a heartbeat. This supremely physical action is not merely mechanical, it is also the body's poetry and rhythm. Life is a complicated and uneven mixture of what is and what the heart wishes it to be, and surely, at some point, even the most seasoned realists long to be lost in the love of an exquisite, unbelievable vision. There is an expression which is common in helping circles, having many variations, but goes something like: if you give a person a fish you satisfy their hunger for a meal but if you teach a person to fish you give them the gift of self-reliance forever. It's a helpful saying, but it's also necessary to remember that fishing, in its essence, is not simply food gathering, it's also an art.

I once spoke with someone who told me that he took off work one afternoon because he had the itch to go fishing. He described the preparations in detail: his precise attention to time and place, sufferance in waiting many long hours for a nibble, and an eloquent description of the fish he finally caught. As he spoke, he touched on all the tangible nuances which give value and measure to life itself: planning, anticipation, expectation, thoughtfulness, patience, and imagination. His final remarks were elegantly to the point, "Good eatin'," he said: he had fulfilled his desire to become one with the fish. Fishing indeed is a soulful venture, and if we are inclined to teach a person to fish, we must allow the person's right to their art of living.

Eventually, both Elmer and the children who came together in that remarkable project moved on and away to another place and time. If, in life, they find a measure of happiness and fulfillment they may do so by remembering the birdhouse incident. They may even ponder that the same steadfast skill they together used to build an elegant house for birds, was, in fact, the exact artistry which eventually brought them an uncommon and abiding fulfillment in all life.

Sophocles, Seagulls, and Success

Listen! you hear the grating roar
Of pebbles which the waves draw back, and fling,
At their return, up the high strand,
Begin, and cease, and then again begin,
With tremulous cadence slow, and bring
The eternal note of sadness in.
Sophocles long ago heard it on the Aegean...

MATTHEW ARNOLD, *Dover Beach*

I thank whatever Gods may be
for my unconquerable soul.

WILLIAM ERNEST HENLEY, *Invictus*

Begin again

We sat on a bench, two aging children of the 1960's, at the edge of the beach looking out at the ocean. It was a warm summer's evening on the road to Cape May, New Jersey, sometime around 2004, moonlit and fresh with a gentle sea breeze. We were resting after a long bike ride, and we soon began to talk about the projects in which we had both been involved over the years and how difficult the struggle had been to realize youthful hopes and ideals.

Ken Smith and I came to know each other in the mid-1980s when he was working with emergency housing services for the Salvation Army, and I was heavily involved with the organization of Friendship House as a homeless resource center. A firestorm of controversy surrounded the project when the city of Wilmington, Delaware, objecting to the use of portable heaters, closed our emergency winter shelter, a converted thrift store, and we were struggling to find places for those who were now out on the street.

From out of nowhere, Ken phoned to ask if the Salvation Army canteen truck would be of any help. I was surprised by the generosity of his offer, even mildly flabbergasted; it was so unexpected and sincere. Then and there we became friends and over the years we've done a lot of work together.

There are some deep pitfalls in community work, along with endless discouragements and heartaches. The effort to establish new programs is difficult enough, even without their innovative elements which stir negative emotions as when the realm of charity clashes with that of social justice. Sadly, even among the most altruistic there is often a lot of pride, selfishness, jealousy, and fight for territory: on the bright side there is the sheer, uncompromising passion which motivates such persons, while on the dull side, like thirsty snarling critters at the shrinking oasis, there is the ever-present competitive quest for funding.

After we had finished venting a quarter century of steam, we sat more quietly in the still of the evening discussing our mutual desires and efforts which, over the years, have come and gone, re-evaluating with humor some of the more wrenching and embarrassing failures in the gentler light of hindsight. Recalling some of our visions for social change, we wondered why more could not have been achieved, and why injustice, albeit in many new and subtle forms, seems ever revitalized and hopelessly entrenched in human affairs.

As we spoke, and the longer we sat, I became aware of two prevailing and persistent sounds: the rhythmic rolling of the ocean, more ancient than Sophocles, and the intrusive, blunt squawking of the sea gulls. These scavengers, even in their unrelenting pizza-Kabuki-dance with vacationers, are as timeless as the sea itself. Even as we sat discussing what seemed like such weighty matters, I realized that both sea and sea gulls would long outlast our conversation; their song and screech extending year after year, century after century into the distant ages. So is the eternity of the life inside us: it lasts forever.

The Victorian poet Matthew Arnold laments the cultural decline of a once surging wave of faith: he sees a world without certainty as in sad defeat and without hope, like the ocean, once mighty in full tide, now retreating in un-heroic ebb. Struggling in vain to change the world apart from the certitude of who we are, we find no success, and the universe proceeds on through millennia, impassive to our feeble bluster, as our frantic efforts to change things fizzle: a once potent effervescence of effort, now flat in time.

What then keeps us going, when it would be so easy to despair and give up? The moment in time we have to make a difference is so brief and the obstacles are so everlastingly stubborn: yet there is an optimism lit inside us to we know we can never give up, even if what passes for worldly success eludes us. Sophocles took the melancholy of a receding Aegean as like the tragedy of fate in the human story, but the sea itself is impassive: while it may mirror the heart of sadness that is not the whole story. It also reflects the grandeur of an eternal affection of which we human beings are heirs.

As the ocean current is irresistible, so is the sea of life inside us, our source. There is no higher morality than that we belong to one another. Life, like the ocean, knows nothing of death, only unending change: always to grow, beyond the confines of dogma and the falsehoods of certainty. For in that final turn, the righteousness of a lifetime dissolves, and what we wanted to achieve with such fervent desire was always there, within ourselves, only asking the courage to know it. Like the limitless waves which make the world one, so our belief and hope is fixed. Our commitment, after all, is not to a trinket of cultural success, but to the timeless unchanging oneness of all people. The life within us is indeed unconquerable. Perhaps real success is finally to apprehend the true extent of who we already are.

Anatomy of a First Step

Take the first step in faith. You don't have to see the whole staircase, just take the first step.

MARTIN LUTHER KING, JR.

There are two mistakes one can make along the road to truth... not going all the way, and not starting.

SIDDHARTHA GAUTAMA [Buddha]

A small audacity

It has been said that the secret of the ancient rite of fire-walking is not in surviving the burning coals, but in deciding to go ahead, to take the first step: such is the power inherent in a decision to begin a journey. Uncertainty and fear keep us from that first step and the thought of leaving a secure place. If these are our only considerations, we'd never move; something else challenges us to lay these aside, let go of the weight of self-doubt and incapacitating fear, and travel forward toward things unknown. It's our own happiness we seek, the excitement of growth, to travel into the undiscovered places of our soul, and to find ourselves in others. It's what Jesus, in his unequivocal insistence to leave all behind, was always asking his followers to do: teaching that truth is not enshrined in boneyards, but only in the tumult of life, all life as we dare to know it, and as we unlock its mysteries we find ourselves reborn. The most sacred decision of a lifetime is to take a first step, to begin a voyage, toward a horizon on the other side of which may be the end of our well-known world.

Sean was an eight-year-old boy who, with his mother and younger sister, lived for several weeks in the winter emergency shelter in 2011. He was to all appearances a typical boy, energetic and curious; he and his sister adroitly darting among the grownups to get into the supper line first, or be at hand as soon as snacks were put out at night. He was also shy and quiet, more so perhaps because he had a severe speech stutter. A stammer like his is more than a simple impediment: it is a debilitating and embarrassing deformity of social interchange and it literally cripples the soul and personality into a timid withdrawal from others. Like in the Movie, *The King's Speech*, the rise of a monarch along with the fate of an empire might hang on such a thing as this humiliating defect of speech. We assumed Sean always to be a pleasant kid, except abjectly timid and not to be asked to talk; even to tell you his name was an agonizing ordeal. Imagine, then, our astonishment when, as we crowded into the dining area before supper and the leader asked for a volunteer to say grace, Sean stood up from the group, came forward, and offered to pray.

Not even a whisper, but absolute quiet prevailed as he stammered through the first words, and continued with halting and persevering courage to speak on everyone's behalf—struggling yet persistent—to a riveted assemblage. When he finished it seemed the room itself jumped to its feet, every last person smiling and applauding wildly. Sean was radiant, red-faced and alive with the pride of his achievement. However the words of his halting prayer moved us, the stunning inspiration was when he first so slowly stood, seemingly from out of nowhere, and took that first step to the front. All eyes were transfixed on him and with good reason: whoever we were, homeless or housed, we were, each of us, walking with him, vicariously reveling in his courage. Never has grace before a meal been more celebrated!

Where did Sean find the heart to do something so utterly impossible, to leave his secure place of inconspicuous and contented silence in the moment before he stood up? Perhaps it was as uncomplicated as to know with certainty he was among friends. He was in a place where people believed in and liked him; not so much the hallowed environ of a church building, as in the truly sacred space of a neighborhood of persons who cared enough to want to know him. The enigma of why anyone would be so daring in the face of the unknown can be unraveled in the ease of a smile, a meeting of eyes, a sincere hand extended. In this place, Sean found the audacity to stand.

At the instant our uncertain stride becomes sure footing, our hesitation ends and we know that we belong to ourselves again. Possibilities flower ahead of us. It may be from the confidence of others, or in our own trust, that we step onto the ship to begin the crossing to the unknown shore. Whatever the reasons, that gutsy step may be the first of hundreds more on the voyage to that shining place we imagined when we first wondered what was on the other side.

Conclusion: A Least Expected Heaven

Religion without humanity is very poor human stuff.

SOJOURNER TRUTH

When I first saw Marsha Young at the College bookstore, I knew. She was a captivating beauty, and I was from tip to toe taken with her. It must have been her hazel eyes, I think; they seemed to smile all by themselves. She was eighteen, tall, slender, and long-legged like someone fond of running. She wore jeans and a faded army shirt, shirttails out, looking for all the world like the army brat I later learned she was. She carried herself quietly, as if there were no one else in the store, serenely scanning the shelves of books, picking and glancing into one, then another; I hoped she might look my way, just for a second, but she didn't. I took my chance to approach her, not yet having the courage to risk meeting but artfully positioning myself behind her in the checkout line. It was bliss to be that close, but to no avail. She made her purchase and left.

It was the summer of 1971, and I had enrolled in Nyack College in New York to finish my undergraduate degree. After first seeing Marsha, I was more determined than ever to meet her, and I finally got my chance a few days later in the cafeteria at breakfast. She was sitting at a large round table with a group of friends, and I nonchalantly took one of the empty seats. This time she noticed and asked my name. As luck would have it, I mentioned that I was driving into New York City on the weekend, and that got her interest. Trying desperately to keep my cool, I casually said that if she wanted to come she would be welcome, and, with my insides leaping for joy, we made the date. Two years later on June 10, 1973 we were married at Ramapo Presbyterian Church in Suffern, New York.

She was my partner in life for 35 years and never stopped

reminding me of the summer breeze I felt when I first saw her. In our years with the Meeting Ground community, we learned the toughest side of love: the ability to work together. She herself was the gift, and she taught me much about what meeting and embracing others in truth meant. She could easily be holding a friend's hand at three in the morning, raptly listening to the culmination of a betrayal or the despair of a letdown. She once planted herself by the lonely beside of a homeless women dying in, of all places, a motel room. She kept vigil with her non-stop for days until the end of her life, and continued to speak warmly of what reverence for the life-force she found in that relationship.

When I finished seminary in 1978, we moved to Springfield, Massachusetts where I pastored a small, struggling congregation, one of the rare Presbyterian churches in New England where they like to keep their religion in local hands. We were there for three years, and we loved the people of Christ Church, but we were restless to follow another drummer, the one calling to begin a new kind of fellowship, a Meeting Ground. The whole idea was one humongous risk. We had to pull up stakes, move to Maryland and figure a way to get started. Marsha and I struggled big time over that one. Our daughter was two years old, we had little savings, and we both left secure jobs to start over from scratch; not just to support ourselves but find a way to make the idea of Meeting Ground believable. That first step was the hardest. Believe me, there were times late at night when we agonized over what we could possibly be thinking. Come morning though, the dream was always still intact, and the horizon didn't look as daunting; once we took ship, the voyage took us to a new world and changed us in ways we never imagined.

Marsha died of cancer on May 12, 2008: too soon, too young; she took a still unfinished part of me with her. I miss our working together; I even miss the troubled times. Strange how memory softens the past so that even the arguments and standoffs become, like the tedious trials of learning to ride a bike, bittersweet and fond recollections. We once had a strong disagreement on how to assist a homeless mother who had told us the remarkable yet doubtful story that she was raised in a Catholic orphanage which was located on the site of the former Auschwitz concentration camp. While Marsha was fascinated with this account of her background, I couldn't bring myself to believe it was true. All the research we did proved inconclusive and it came down to a simple matter of accepting or not accepting the face value of what she said.

Marsha proved the better part. She befriended her, not for any details of her past, true or untrue, but for who she was as a person now. I think that quality was the reason people relished visits in her office, which she set up, not in an isolated corner, but right at the front door of Wayfarers' House. She would drop what she was doing to greet visitors, expected or not, with a gigantic smile and an unfailing hug. Somehow, through that and everything else she did, people got the message they were vitally important to know. She loved hearing their stories, and that included everyone, no matter their station or success. She taught me a universe of empathy in listening, not to judge fact or lie, worthy or unworthy, as the person's value was settled in her mind *at hello*; her keen desire was to know, from another person, what she might discover was truest in herself.

Shortly after we were married we took a long walk together on a hot summer's night along the beach in Wildwood, New Jersey. A full moon was rising and casting a brilliant corridor of light across the moving waters and, it seemed, right to where we were. We were wrapped in the brightness. We talked about the future, and our mutual desire to build relationships with and among persons on the forgotten side of life, those living outside a place where most people felt they belonged. Finally, tiring of words, we climbed up into a tall lifeguard seat, and just sat silently watching out into the vast waters of the unknown, knowing somehow, as we all do in those rare gossamer times, that we belonged to it and it to us. I've gone back to that place many times since—to feel again the closeness of the chilled night air and hear the constant, eternal motion of the waters: like the rocking cradle of life itself. There I can continue the conversation in my mind that I began with Marsha 40 years ago.

THERE'S SOMETHING ABOUT THE OCEAN that resonates with our being. When I walk along its edge, I think that against it wealth and power, even religious opinion, count for remarkably little. In its ebb and flow there are no judgments; here there is only the authority of being; here the petty grandeur of institutional religion pales to nothing. In the roll of its waves, we are rocked in the awareness that our meeting, our relationship with all other life, as to ourselves, is indeed our true religion. When I was younger, and like many of my generation, I had high ideals about changing the world, and I believed in the possibility of this transformation. Over the years, I've come around to thinking that I should have put more energy into changing myself, slightly embarrassed still to be learning elementary lessons of life. I've also become certain that the *spirituality of meeting* holds the promise that institutional religion can change, that the church can find new life as it looks outside its rusted canons and inside the people, all manner of people, with whom it would have the boldness to become one.

I suspect it was the sheer energy of the *Risorgimento* that aroused a new spirit of adventure in young Italians coming of age in the wake of that movement. The indelible image of Giuseppe Garibaldi, a hero larger than life itself, marshaling his people with an *élan* only the heart, the eternal restless sea inside us, can know. Waiting the call to wake up and stand on the sunlit shore, hands shading above our eyes, to see in our riveted imagination, not a thin line on the other side of somewhere… but a wondrous place, only reached by daring the sea: the vast ocean which is life itself. My ancestors, and those like them, make me believe it's possible because of their bravery to venture the unknown, to risk all, lose their life, and cross from an old world to a new. That voyage is what I think about when I feel the fear that would beset anyone looking to begin again.

A Ketchup Mandala

SOMETIME AROUND 1984, in our first year at Clairvaux Farm, a mother and her two young children arrived in a broken down jalopy, slowly chugging up the lane trailing a plume of gray smoke. They had packed up everything they owned and somehow, by a thread of the miraculous, driven from Utah looking in vain for a brother somewhere in Maryland with whom they might live. Stranded with no place to go, they got word about the farm and now, in a final heaving heroic gasp, their clunker rolled into our parking lot and gave up the ghost. The inside of the car looked like a hoarder's pantry: clothes, pots and pans, books, shoes, magazines, bric-a-brac, and blankets were crammed everywhere except the hollowed out spaces where the children sat, and any time the space was vacated a small avalanche filled it in. There was even the family dog, a small terrier that had given birth to puppies *en route* across the country.

In those days, before we built a separate dining hall, we ate together in a small room off the farmhouse kitchen, so meals were exceedingly cozy affairs. The first time this new family ate dinner with us, the boy Jeffrey, a withdrawn, unsmiling, and silent seven-year-old stood up in his chair and started to stretch across the table to grab a bottle of ketchup. Unable to quite reach he put one knee on the table and extended his whole body across serving bowls, glasses, dishes; I thought the table itself might give way. His mother and four-year-old sister, sitting beside him, seemed unperturbed and just kept eating, faces in their plates, as if nothing unusual were happening. I can't recall who it was that finally went over to help him out, but in trying to get him off the table and back into his seat, they unwittingly pushed a button that set off a crying tantrum. As he screamed and flailed off the chair to the floor in a fit of frenzy, one after another hastily ended their meal and even his mother gave up on any further effort at dinner.

Now, lest you get the impression this episode was characteristic of all his behavior, I need to say that Jeffrey was, for the most part, unusually passive and quiet, even to the point of appearing unresponsive. These outbursts occurred when he was frustrated by his inability to communicate easily with others; he had no tools to build relationships. Unending homelessness had distracted his mother to the point where everything else, including her children, seemed incidental in the overwhelming struggle to survive. He had never been taught such elementary nuances of human interaction as table manners. He wanted ketchup, he reached for ketchup; what frustrated him so much was that he didn't have enough power in his life to manage even this modest achievement.

In the days and weeks that followed, I made it my goal to try to teach him the technique of getting what he wanted at the table. One basic thing, I thought, that might be the basis of a relationship. It was a slow process. He didn't get it all at once. His language skill was underdeveloped, and he said little except in words and short phrases. Yet slowly I began to see the first hint of change in his eyes. At first looking blankly everywhere but at mine, he began to make fleeting brief contact, then longer, then expressions came, smiling, short-lived at first, but gradually I watched him come to life. In time he learned to stay in his seat at dinner and say, "Please pass the ketchup," and when this happened there was a ripple of affection, not to mention relief, among all at the table.

Jeffrey's family was with us for about three months. I'll never forget the morning they left: all climbing into their patched-up car and starting off down the lane, lumbering up to speed like an old steam locomotive. It suddenly dawned on Jeffrey that this was it; they were leaving, never to return. He began to cry, then bawl with that deep release of sadness which only comes from the gut of a child. Tears streaming down his wet, red face, he reached both arms out the window, extending them as far as he possibly could, then down as if to grab the ground and hold it tightly. Standing, watching, torn apart by his obvious desolation, I felt like Jeffrey, only too adult-controlled to express it with his eloquence. I remember someone once saying that the measure of love we have for someone is most truly voiced in the depth of sorrow expressed in leaving. It's true. The boy and I, along with his family, had grown together.

As the car disappeared down the road and we slowly, sadly began to go about our day, I thought about the ketchup, and somehow the ancient religious *Mandala* came into my head along with it: the archetypal circular symbol which signifies the wholeness of the self, the divinity incarnate in everyone, the *Imago Dei,* image of God of Genesis in which all of us are formed. "How do you like that?" I thought to myself, "I wonder if there is such a thing as a *Ketchup Mandala*?" I had helped Jeffrey find his place at the table where we all gather, and he, mutually, as the eternal wheel turned, helped me to find where heaven is: not surely in the sweet bye and bye, but in the sacred and ageless ancestral circle of who we are now and what we discover about ourselves when we are together. The affection expressed in human meeting is more than coming near to heaven—it is the stunning reminder that a place in the heart is surely dearer to us than a place in the sky.

The Transforming Voyage

My Aunt Norma is among the last surviving family of my childhood: my late mother's youngest sister who, approaching her hundredth birthday, watches the warm sun gently set in Naples, Florida where she lives. In the bridge of my lifetime, her mother Rosa, as a young bride, watched the same sun rise in Naples, Italy as she boarded ship to America, never again to see her birth-land, a country just breaking free of late-19th-century feudalism. Airplanes and automobiles were things only in one's unvoiced dreams and the trans-ocean passage was made by belching steamers, which had only just replaced sailing ships in the fabled Atlantic crossing. Victoria was queen in England, and Theodore Roosevelt was barely out of his teens.

She was an Italian, but she would give birth to children who would only know another homeland. Crossing the ocean was more than a passage from Naples to Philadelphia; it was a voyage of imagination into another universe, an unseen land of hope and hazard. My grandmother may have steeled herself for the journey by thinking, as many did, that it was a temporary trip, that in time she would return to Italy, but it was not to be. At some point, she began to perceive that life was larger than nationality and on the far shore of America she better understood who she was. The life and relationships of a new world were greater than the former rules and confines which once had been her undying pledge. After raising ten children, she went on to become a successful businesswoman and restaurateur, a career she began from scratch when she was already past 60. It was indeed another country, and her youngest daughter today looks out her window on a new Naples: on things far beyond what my young grandmother could, even in her wildest dreams, ever imagine. The journey of those forbears was not a mere transit—it was a reawakening, a *Risorgimento* of their soul. All who made it were unwittingly born again.

I can only begin to wonder what her young mother, my grandmother Rosa, must have thought about as she watched the last of Italy slip below the horizon. Surely there must have been a pricking fear along with a more dreadful hesitation. Was this the right decision? On the near shore was home, as she had ever known it. Beyond the alluring coastline of the sea was the risk of a larger world, a greater home for which she longed, not knowing fully why. Leaving embodied truth, secure and ancient systems, can't be done without a great hesitation. We can revere, even relish, their memory, but knowing ourselves in and through knowing others, and working together to build a neighborhood that never was, is a voyage from which we retreat at the peril of our soul.

A Least Expected Heaven

I can't remember where or when I first heard about heaven. It must have been in church, I think, but I also remember asking my mother about the sky and why it was blue. She may have worked it into the conversation then. Whenever it was, though, I was never quite satisfied with what I was told: that it was a place *up there*, somewhere. A well-meaning and intensely earnest minister once confided to me that he was sure heaven was on the far side of the moon, "or else why would God not show us what the other side looks like?" Makes perfect sense, although with modern advances in astronomy he might now have to imagine that heaven is on the far side of Pluto, or some other place our space machines have yet to photograph. Everyone who seemed to know was unanimous that heaven is a place of bliss where the saved, the good, go when they die. I must tell you that even as a kid the whole thing sounded unreal, what with massive crowds of endlessly courteous church people playing harps with angels, and boring, what with no disagreements or heartbreaks, and never again to know the bittersweet sadness of being disappointed in love. And especially that it was always told to me to be a place of division, an ark of eternal safety, not for everybody—only for some: the elect, the chosen, the saved, the good, the blessed. In this celestial place, I was told, there will be no memory of the excluded, nor capacity for their pity, nor thirst for their mercy. Thinking about it that way, we have to ask: how is that a heaven we even wish to imagine?

The grown-up in us swells up to shout: "Why do we live this way!?" What is it that we want: a place for our everlasting dreamland or a new vista for humanity on earth? Is it not that we want a world in which we fashion human kinship instead of spires and make a difference for others by giving, not so much a year-end donation, but the gift of ourselves. If we want to find heaven it won't be by being good and hoping for the best after we die, and it won't be in the increase of religious charity or misguided attempts to rearrange persons and their lives like furniture in a room. The kingdom of heaven, I have on trustworthy authority, is within us, in the gift of our being and in our sovereign power to make a difference in this world because we meet, we listen to, we accept that we indeed belong to ourselves, and others, and that we are not many, but one. We do, in fact, love our neighbor as ourselves for that same reason.

Jesus did not live and die to found an institution. However organized religion prides itself as the repository of his corporate memory, it is, first and last, a conscious human invention, as all such industrial organisms created to give shape to our waking lives. If we live in dread of what might be said of us for believing that God lives within us, known in the sovereignty of our relationships, and not on the ceiling of St. Peter's Basilica; if we are resigned to paying the dear price of relinquishing the image our own divinity to the exigencies of religion, and relying on a future garden of lush vindication for our trouble, then maybe we are right to hope for a pearl-lined avenue somewhere in the pious hereafter. But we can never divide ourselves into those who belong and those who don't. Our merit is not in the kingdom that is to come, but in the creation of neighborhood with each other, among all, and the rising of human communion that overruns, not to a place in the sky someday, but the green and lush heart we share as people here on earth: a heaven we least expected.

And I know, even as I found myself captivated in a college bookstore, that the land of our future is here, in the present, today, right now where we are. Heaven, as our breath, is among us. As we belong to ourselves, to one another, and to all living, so that identity, that ownership, is one. Outside religion, there is the mercy seat of being and the hallowed thing spoken is the unassailable dogma of who you and I, in truth, are.

We may yet finally yield that the ark of safety is not a sterile golden paradise at the end of a road straightly mapped by priests. All along we have been better guided by the conscience we meet along the circle, ever coming around like the springtime memory of a smile we can never forget, ever recalling us to a promised land we can only find together: to our yet unawakened dream, and to the everlasting foundations unveiled in those timeless moments when you and I were not apart.   Ω

Appendix

This book is not meant to be a chronological history of Meeting Ground, but a brief outline of Meeting Ground's history to date might be helpful in better understanding the stories that are related to it.

1981 – 1982: Meeting Ground founded. Wayfarers' House opens in Elkton, Maryland as a community for women, men, and families experiencing homelessness.

1983 – Clairvaux Farm opens in Earleville, Maryland (12 miles south of Elkton) as a community primarily for families with children, but also women and men. Wayfarers' House becomes a community for homeless women and their children.

1985 – 1986: Meeting Ground founds Friendship House in Wilmington, Delaware as a thrift store and daytime help center for persons living on the streets in the surrounding neighborhood. During a severe winter storm homeless persons begin to sleep there overnight, and the city orders the makeshift shelter closed for violating fire safety regulations (operating an unauthorized heater). Friendship House is then reorganized, under Meeting Ground's leadership, as a partnership of Delaware faith communities and reopened in a new location.

1986: Meeting Ground leads in organizing the Border Outreach Project, assisting those in Tucson Arizona in the Sanctuary Movement, working to aid political and economic refugees from Central America. Within two years the project evolves, under Rick Ufford-Chase, to BorderLinks, a peace and justice educational project.

1990: Meeting Ground leads a partnership that establishes Settlement House in Elkton Maryland, a community for men, especially veterans who are experiencing homelessness.

2006: Meeting Ground organizes a winter church-based emergency shelter in Cecil County, Maryland, rotating weekly among area churches. The shelter houses up to 45 persons including families with children, women, and men.

2008: Marsha Mazza dies of cancer at age 55. She was the co-founder of Meeting Ground and the person who established and directed Wayfarers' House as a unique community for women.

18911372R00084

Made in the USA
Lexington, KY
01 December 2012